WELDING ANOTHER LINK

WELDING ANOTHER LINK

Latter-day Saint Essays on Faith and Intellect

Nathan B. Oman

GREG KOFFORD BOOKS
SALT LAKE CITY

Copyright © 2026 Nathan B. Oman.
Cover design copyright © 2026 Greg Kofford Books, Inc.
Cover design by Loyd Isao Ericson.

Published in the USA.

All rights reserved. No part of this volume may be reproduced in any form without written permission from the publisher, Greg Kofford Books. The views expressed herein are the responsibility of the authors and do not necessarily represent the position of Greg Kofford Books.

ISBN: 978-1-58958-837-0
Also available in ebook.

Greg Kofford Books
P. O. Box 1362
Draper, UT 84020
www.gregkofford.com
facebook.com/gkbooks
twitter.com/gkbooks

Library of Congress Control Number: 2026934895

For my parents.

Contents

Foreword

James E. Faulconer

An important question for many Latter-day Saints is how, as individuals, they relate to the Church as an institution and a community: how do the particularities of a person's individual faith life relate to the universalism of the gospel? How is the Church's history in the western United States relevant to a South American, African, Asian, or European member? Can one be faithful but reject some teachings of the Church in the past? In the present? How does a person respond to the darker aspects we find in scripture: infanticide, genocide, racism? How do we reconcile our religious life with the fact that, simultaneously, we live in the secular world?

As Nathan Oman reminds us, the answer cannot be found unless we recognize the conceptual framework within which such questions arise. Thinkers like Charles Taylor have pointed out the supposed decline of religion that began in earnest in the twentieth century is not really a decline. Rather, it is a change in the conditions of belief: first, the idea that we can understand the world in human-centered terms, without reference to transcendence but also without rejecting it. (Taylor calls this "the immanent frame.") Second, the growth of individualism. Third, the understanding of the good in terms of human flourishing rather than in terms of a transcendent good. The world of secularity is not defined by unbelief but by plurality: faith is always possible though not necessary. Faith is optional, so it is necessarily contested and fragile.

My response to these kinds of questions has been to look to the embodied character of the Father and the Son and their relations as showing us what it means to be related to them. Each member of the Godhead is who he is only in embodied covenant relation with each other member, as well as in relation with the children of the Father. On that view the ultimate goal of human existence for Latter-day Saints—Zion or the Kingdom of God—is a function of the constellations of the relationships that are created among God's children. In imitation of the relations of the Godhead, we form covenants, covenants of family relations, understood broadly, and covenants of friendship.[1] In covenant these relations continue coming to be; they are not static. They are divine covenant relations guaranteed by God's and our continuing faithfulness to one another rather than by some unembodied, non-relational metaphysical power or authority. To use Oman's own words for describing my position, the Kingdom of God comes to be through covenant relations that create (and continue to create) a welding link between all of God's children.

In personal terms, this means that we can be faithful only because we find ourselves in an ongoing, historically established set of relations, rather than formal ones. Our relations with one another do not arise out of nowhere. We have them only because we are always already in relation with God and others. These ongoing relations create a non-metaphysical changing "whole" of individuals in covenant relations that grounds our possibilities for understanding and acting. That historical and ever-changing ground of relational covenant is the ground of faith, whether we find ourselves born into relations that have been built on that ground and which we inherit, or we are brought into them through conversion.

The tension religious people encounter is between that framework or ground for life in the world, and the secular framework within which religious life finds itself. That is religion's tension with a framework that is usually merely indifferent to religion but sometimes hostile to it. In various ways, the essays in this book take on the question of what that tension between religious and secular life means for faithful Latter-day Saints.

Oman is not only one of the most distinguished scholars of religion and law in the United States, he is also the premier Latter-day Saint thinker looking at our history and culture through the lens of the law, particularly common law. Oman knows the US Constitution and law more generally quite well. He is a clear writer. He makes careful, clear-eyed arguments, assuming that he is at least headed in the right direction but not insisting that his views are authoritative. He recognizes his own fallibility but is unafraid to argue for what he believes. Perhaps most importantly, in these essays, Oman writes not just for other scholars of the law but for any thoughtful Latter-day Saint, without regard for their educational degree.

Looking at the table of contents, even with the division made between essays related to faith and others related to intellect, a reader might be forgiven for not seeing a thread running through the collection of essays

1. I use the term *covenant* to refer not only to the formal covenants we enter into via the institutional church but also to the innate covenant we have with all others because we are God's children.

as a whole. But this is not just a random collection. In my reading of these essays, their guiding thread is the necessity (to paraphrase Oman slightly) for a Latter-day Saint intellectual to gain "a conviction that the core claims of divine restoration through Joseph Smith are true and, more importantly, [to become] convinced of the requirement that [the person] live life in light of that conviction."[2] Mormonism—a way of living more than a set of beliefs—must be the structuring basis on which the person's life rests, even as it lives in unavoidable tension with the immanent frame. In the end, it turns out that the thread that connects these essays is not just a thread. More than that, it works to weld another link in the chain of wonder at the Restoration.

I must confess that Oman and I see the world in largely similar ways, which is probably why he asked me to write this foreword. Yet, though I recognize that this is largely a collection of previously published or presented pieces, I wish that Oman had edited them to make their guiding thread more explicit. Each of these essays is excellent, though I must confess that because of my personal temperament I was much more drawn to those in the first section and to the final essay.

That said, this is one of the best collections of essays on Latter-day Saint faith—especially for those in their twenties and thirties who are bothered by the kinds of questions I mentioned at the beginning, questions of how to remain faithful in a world that sees faith quite differently than do the faithful.

Read on!

2. Page 10 herein.

FAITH

CHAPTER 1

A Local Faith

On October 22, 1844, men and women across America were disappointed when the world did not come to an end. They were the followers of a lay Baptist preacher named William Miller. Beginning in 1833, Miller, a native of New York's Burned-over District, began producing elaborate biblical commentaries indicating that Christ's Second Coming was imminent. Working with these writings, his followers converged on October 22 as the day of the Savior's coming, much to their ultimate disappointment.

Mormonism might easily have suffered a similar fate. Indeed, in 1843, as excitement over Miller's predictions was reaching its height, Joseph Smith told of a revelation informing him that he would see the Lord face to face if he lived to be eighty-five years old. "I was left thus," he said, "without being able to decide whether this coming referred to the beginning of the millennium or to some previous appearing, or whether I should die and thus see his face" (D&C 130:16). This coy prophecy, however, was an outlier. In contrast to the Millerites, the promised Millennium of Mormonism was less a moment than a place—Zion, the New Jerusalem—to be built up to the Lord by the gathering of the faithful. Mormonism thus made connection to a particular location a central element of religious experience. Zion, however, consisted of more than merely the transposition of apocalyptic expectations from time to space. It was a concrete community with neighbors, social halls, neatly laid-out lots, and due allowance for grazing livestock. At its worst, this concept of Zion reduced religion to the mere hum of work and business. At its best, Zion sanctified the ordinary, turning one's home and town into the beachhead of eternity.

The Mormons had their own disappointed expectations. Those disappointments, however, were geographic rather than chronological. The constant need to alter and reinterpret the geography of Zion—as the Saints lost, in succession, promised lands in Ohio, Missouri, and Illinois—left its mark on Mormon doctrine. Even the ultimate resting place in Deseret proved chancy. In 1857, as Johnston's Army marched west to crush the Mormon rebellion, Brigham Young made contingency plans to abandon Utah and move the Saints en masse to the north. The move proved unnecessary, but it took a while for Salt Lake City to become Zion. In the end, however, the force of time and population gave Deseret a theological heft in its own right, and Isaiah's prophecy of the mountain of the Lord's house in the tops of the mountains (Isa. 2:2) was appropriated for the spires of the Salt Lake Temple.

I grew up in the place created by this transposition of the Millennium from time to space. My earliest memories are of the house where I lived as a small child. It was a modest home, built around 1900 in what was then a residential suburb of Salt Lake City. The house stands on Sixth East, between Eighth and Ninth South, the streets measuring themselves from the Salt Lake Temple. During the nineteenth century, this bit of the valley was known as Mill Farm and belonged to Brigham Young. Today, Brigham's farm is a park, and my sister and I played on a swing set in what had been the prophet's backyard. As a child, however, I measured the religious content of my place not from the temple or Brigham's farm, but from a small gazebo set in the middle of the road several blocks north of our house. The Latter-day Saints designed their Zion with wide streets, wide enough to completely turn a wagon and team without unhitching them. It made for roads rather too large for modern residential neighborhoods, with the result that down the middle of the streets ran broad, grassy medians. The gazebo sat on one of these medians surrounded by a modest garden. A small bronze plaque declared that when the Latter-day Saint pioneers entered the valley in July 1847, the only tree growing on the plain before them stood on this spot.

My earliest sense of the sacred emanated from that gazebo. Riding my bike down the tree-lined streets of Salt Lake City, I knew that this wooded world of roads and houses had once been a barren expanse of sagebrush. Driving through the desolate valleys north of Salt Lake City each summer on the way to my grandparents' home in southern Idaho, I could imagine the landscape before the Latter-day Saints arrived. It had been transformed, I was taught, by pioneer-dug irrigation ditches. (My cousins in Utah Valley, fifty miles to the south, still had an irrigation ditch running in front of their house; I was deeply envious.) The green around me had been the pioneers' dream, a desert blossoming as a rose, according to prophecy (Isa. 35:1).

In the chapel where we attended church each Sunday was a vast stained-glass window portraying Joseph Smith's First Vision. My father still has the drawing of it that I produced during one of the long, boring meetings filled with unremembered sermons. At the window's center, Joseph kneels before two hovering figures in white. One gestures toward the other. Green glass depicting the leaves of the Sacred Grove surrounds them. In my mind, the glowing leaves in the window merged with the sacred greenery of Salt

Lake City. Just as the presence of God sanctified the leaves surrounding Joseph, stories of barren valleys, pioneers, and the arboreal redemption they wrought sanctified the trees of my childhood. I lived in God's city, not a place as sacred as where Joseph had his theophany but a place nevertheless touched by God's cosmic plan. When I received my first Bible, I turned to the passages in Isaiah on the mountain of the Lord's house and the blossoming rose of the desert and marked them with a red pencil.

At eight years old, I was baptized. Our chapel did not have a baptismal font. Rather, we made our way six blocks west and eight blocks north to Temple Square. I recall standing before a bronze statue of handcart pioneers. To me, their struggle across the continent seemed the epitome of righteous heroism. My father informed me that my own ancestors had pulled such handcarts to Zion in the mid-nineteenth century. Next to the statue stood Brigham Young's great Tabernacle. My father pointed to its domed roof and explained how the lattice of rafters was held together by rawhide lashings and what a marvel the building had been when it first rose in the 1860s. Had the pioneers who lashed together the Tabernacle pulled handcarts as well? They must have, I thought. The building took on their heroism, the heroism of God's chosen Saints doing His will amid a persecuting world. In the basement of the building was a font, and it was there that I went into the waters of baptism and became a Latter-day Saint.

By then Mormonism had long since given up on the geographic gathering to an Intermountain Zion. Indeed, in my childhood during the 1980s, the excitement that my father carried home from Church headquarters, where he worked, was the excitement of a globalizing religion. The glory of Zion was no longer in wagon trains heading west for Utah but in Mormon congregations growing in Latin America, West Africa, and the Philippines. Yet for me, even this global story was tied to the older theology of place. The prophets went forth from Salt Lake City, where the streets were still measured from the temple. Satellites beamed their teachings every six months from the conferences held in the Tabernacle where I was baptized. Even in a global church, my faith was local, tied to the place where I was born.

Eventually I discovered that the town I grew up in is not the center of the world. When I got older, I left Salt Lake City. I lived in other cities that aspired to be the axis mundi: Boston, which Oliver Wendell Holmes declared in his famous "Autocrat of the Breakfast Table" essays to be the hub of the solar system, and Washington, DC, which in the age of the Pax Americana is a city with an honest claim to be the capital of the world. The Salt Lake City of my childhood shrank in size, and as I turned down Pennsylvania Avenue toward the White House or up Massachusetts Avenue toward Harvard Square, I recognized that my hometown could look provincial and unschooled.

With a growing awareness of the vastness of the world beyond Salt Lake City, I realized that my local faith created three temptations. First was the temptation of embracing the cosmic story of my hometown too tightly. The vices of giving in to such a temptation are easy to see and imagine. If Salt Lake City is the axis mundi, the point at which God speaks to prophets for mankind, then perhaps Salt Lake City is the destiny of the world. Much as I love the city, it is not an entirely inspiring vision. For example, if I were to embrace such a view, the two years I spent teaching the message of the Restoration in the cities and towns of Kyoung Sang Do province would become a quixotic attempt to transform Koreans into suburban Utah Latter-day Saints. My mission would be reduced to a project partaking of both a hubristic imperialism and a comic parochialism. Likewise, my local faith could easily become smug, ignorantly content in its own self-importance. My locality would be the hub of the solar system without Holmes's redeeming irony. The result would be a narrow and sterile life that suffers all the more from not knowing that it is narrow and sterile.

The second temptation was to embrace the cosmopolitan world of Boston and Washington, DC. From this perch, Utah could be dismissed as a colorful backwater, perhaps an interesting place to be from but one that needn't make strong spiritual claims. My local faith could be transformed into a kind of nostalgia. The vocabulary for such a self-understanding lay ready-made. Mormonism could become my "heritage" or my "tradition," a marker of identity in a modern world that understands such markers to be secondary to the more universal claims of democracy, meritocracy, and pop culture. I could transform Mormonism into a repository from which to selectively take materials for my self-authored identity. It would no longer claim me. Rather, I would appropriate the colorful or fashionable bits of it to create a persona, one tied to the Mormon stories of place but only as a literary conceit. I could become like the law school classmate who waxed eloquent on the virtues of his picturesque Mormon childhood while sipping coffee and other forbidden gentile beverages with aspiring citizens of the cosmopolis. For all its occasional hypocrisy, the cosmopolitan world is a tolerant place and likes nothing better than a bit of local color, provided that the local remains firmly subjugated to the cosmopolitan. The leaves of my childhood, however, were not simply colorful. They were sacred.

In a sense, the scandal of my local faith, of a spirituality reared in Salt Lake City as the center of the world, is simply the hometown version of a common scandal. How can that which is local make claims that are universal? Jesus was an itinerant Jewish preacher in a provincial backwater who claimed to be the son of God, the Word made flesh in Nazareth, of all places. The paradox, it would seem, is that all life, including religious life, is local, endowed with a set of particularities arising from history, place, and tradition. It is these particularities to which we are necessarily attached. Inevitably we live in a particular place, a particular time, and a particular history. The appeal of the religious particularities of my childhood, however, lay precisely in the hope that they offered something beyond themselves. The trees and streets and tabernacles and temples formed a chain leading from my bicycle on the sidewalks of Sixth East back through time and space and myth and revelation to God.

It is here that I faced a third temptation. It was the temptation to abandon the particularities and reach only for that which is beyond them. It was the temptation to give up—out of embarrassment at its locatedness—a faith that is somewhere and reach instead for an unlocated faith that is nowhere in particular. A universal faith shorn of particularities offers the hope of being unencumbered by the local. It is an attractive vision, one in which I might enjoy the spiritual riches of the Restoration without its scandalous details. In short, perhaps I can avoid the burden of a sacred story enmeshed in the parochial streets of Salt Lake City.

My Mormonism, however, teaches me that there is a kind of nihilism in the universal. The point shows up most powerfully in the Latter-day Saint concept of God. For example, Orson Pratt, one of our great nineteenth-century thinkers and polemicists, attacked the traditional vision of a God without body, parts, or passions. He wrote: "There are two classes of Atheists in the world. One class denies the existence of God in the most positive language: the other denies his existence in duration or space. One says, 'There is no God;' the other says, 'God is not here or there, any more than he exists now and then.' . . . The infidel says, God does not exist anywhere. The Immaterialist says, 'He exists Nowhere.'"[1] According to Pratt, Mormonism's response to both forms of atheism was to assert the existence of a radically embodied and situated God. "The Father has a body of flesh and bones as tangible as a man's" (D&C 130:22) taught Joseph Smith. It is a doctrine that is not without its own scandals, but it offers the

1. Orson Pratt, *The Essential Orson Pratt*, edited by David J. Whittaker (Signature Books, 1991), 77.

hope of a God who can be approached without an annihilation of the defining particularities of history, space, and body. Indeed, it is striking that Pratt associates atheism with a God shorn of place—"The Immaterialist says, 'He exists Nowhere.'" Even faith needs to be situated someplace.

In the end, it is very difficult to live nowhere in particular, despite the embarrassments of a local faith. Repudiating Salt Lake City would mean giving up a world of sacredness that was given by the landscape of my birth and reaching for a sacredness that was not given to me, one that would have to be self-authored. The problem of a self-authored faith, however, is that ultimately I would confront only myself. Given the human tendency toward self-deception, this would be no mean feat. There is a dignity in self-discovery through a self-created spirituality, but such is not a spirituality in which one sees the face of God amid irrigation ditches and trees planted on the floor of a dusty, sagebrush-covered valley.

I no longer live in Salt Lake City. It has been many years since I left. I now live in the tidewater of eastern Virginia. From time to time, I feel the stab of exile. The James River will transform itself into the waters of Babylon, and I will pledge the cunning of my right hand (Ps. 137:5) not to forget the mountain of the Lord in the tops of the mountains and the gazebo with the plaque remembering the only tree in the valley. I find, however, that even in a landscape dominated by stories of revolution and civil war, my Mormonism can become local. I discover that during the 1840s, Tazwell County, Virginia, had a thriving cluster of Latter-day Saint branches dubbed Little Nauvoo. I ferret out stories of nineteenth-century Latter-day Saints passing through Norfolk on their way from Europe to Zion. I savor the inscription of Latter-day Saint scriptures on the stone exteriors of Virginia and Washington, DC, chapels built in the 1930s and 1940s as part of Mormonism's permanent return to the East Coast. I learn of the great wave of Latter-day Saints brought to the tidewater by war and the US Navy in the 1940s and the birth of our wards and stakes. Even in Virginia, Mormonism can leave its traces on my landscape. My hunger for these details strikes many of my fellow Latter-day Saints as odd, a strange bit of religious pedantry. With them, however, I remain within the sacred world that was given to me as a little boy on Sixth East, and I can plant trees in the spot of ground where God continues to gather me.

CHAPTER 2

From Scandal to Wonder

Mormonism is a scandalous religion. The word scandal comes from the Greek term σκάνδαλον (skandalon). In the New Testament, it is translated as "stumbling block." The central scandal of Mormonism lies in the outlandish claims it makes about its own origins: angels and visions, gold plates and miraculous translations, men claiming to speak with the authority of God. My parents are descended from nineteenth-century Latter-day Saint pioneers, and I cannot recall a time when I did not attend Mormon services and activities each week. Accordingly, I only became gradually aware of Mormonism's scandalousness. It is not that I discovered new facts that had been hidden from me. Indeed, my parents were active participants in scholarly discussions of Mormonism, and I grew up in houses stuffed to overflowing with books on Mormon esoterica. Rather, over the course of my teens and early twenties I came to understand how fanciful the core claims of Mormonism—the ones made week in and week out in Sunday School classes and sacrament meetings—must seem to those not reared within the faith. As I acquired the capacity to see my own religion through the eyes of another, the core story of the Restoration became my stumbling block.

I have never doubted that there is a God. To be sure, I believe that there are plausible reasons for rejecting the existence of God. I studied philosophy as an undergraduate, and I can articulate the objections to the classical philosophical arguments in favor of theism. Indeed, I find many of these objections compelling. Still, try as I might, I have been unable to make atheism a viable alternative in my life. I can't help but experience the world as a creation of God. It is not that I see a beautiful sunset, a crashing ocean, or a stunning mountain range as evidence in support of an argument whose conclusion is "There is a God." Rather, it is that before the beauty of creation, my reflexive reaction is gratitude to God. I can only suppress this response by a conscious act of will. Unless I affirmatively remind myself to think and believe as an atheist, I believe in God. This may be no more than the work of habits instilled at an early age, an ingrained mental tick that turns naturally toward theism. I have no *a priori* reason for supposing that it isn't. Nevertheless, I find myself as a believer, and ultimately I assume that the soundness of my faith will be revealed less in the story of my psychology than in the outcome of the life that my faith has led me to wager.

Unlike a life of atheism, I am quite capable of disbelieving Mormonism. Indeed, in my late teens and early twenties I had bouts of intense doubt about Joseph Smith and the Book of Mormon. While there was one night when I prayed over my doubts and felt a flood of light and fire, it would be a mistake to tell my story in terms of a dramatic resolution of my questions. Indeed, many of my questions remain and over the years I have added some new ones. What came out of my experiences, however, was a commitment to Mormonism. I gained a conviction that the core claims of divine restoration through Joseph Smith were true and, more importantly, I became convinced of the requirement that I live my life in light of that conviction. Mormonism became more than a genealogical identity or an exercise in nostalgia for a pioneer past. Rather, it is the structuring basis for how I choose to live my life.

Today, I find that angst over the scandal of Mormonism has largely disappeared from my spiritual life. I continue to have doubts and questions, but they no longer seem to have existential implications. I am a believing Latter-day Saint, and I don't expect that to change. Rather, I find that the scandal of Mormonism has, for me, taken an ironic and even mischievous turn. Mormonism has become scandalous in the sense of being audacious, exciting, and iconoclastic. Within the largely secular world of the academy, I like to think that being a Latter-day Saint gives me a certain strangeness or edge. (At least to the extent that someone as bland as a law professor can have an edge.) With this rising confidence has come a shift in the sorts of questions that I direct at my faith. Questions such as "Was Joseph Smith a prophet?" or "Is the Book of Mormon true?" are increasingly replaced by questions such as "What does it mean for Joseph Smith to be a prophet?" or "What is the Book of Mormon saying?" Having committed myself to the truth of Mormonism, I find I am more interested in discovering its meaning than continually reevaluating that act of commitment.

As an academic, I am a scholar of the common law. This is the vast corpus developed over the centuries by English and American judges that provides the basic rules of contract, property, and personal security. My legal studies have deepened my appreciation for Mormonism. It is not that my religion provides me with a set of neatly prepackaged answers to the endless succession of difficult choices that the law presents. It does not. Rather, studying the common law has given me a set of mental habits for thinking about my religion. Over the centuries, the common law has attracted a fair bit of intellectual tongue-clicking. T. E. Holland, a nineteenth-century legal intellectual, for example, derided the common law as "chaos with a full index." Upon closer study, however, the common law has a subtle grasp of human nature and a complex internal order that belies the critics who see it as little more than a succession of historical accidents. Out of the welter of seemingly unrelated particular cases emerges something of great usefulness and even beauty.

Mormonism is, by historical standards, a very young religion, and when compared to the elaborate and subtle intellectual traditions that one finds, for example, within Catholicism or Islam, it seems disorganized and underdeveloped. For me, however, this is what lends my faith its intellectual excitement. To be a Latter-day Saint scholar is to stand on the threshold of a great adventure. Only rarely in human history is anyone vouchsafed the opportunity to be present at the birth of a new religious tradition, and while Mormonism is more than a century and a half old, that is, in historical terms, still new. My faith, however, is that Mormonism has the resources to grapple with the most difficult problems of life and mind. Like the common law, the apparently disorganized welter of Mormonism offers great intellectual opportunities to those who are willing to approach it with charity and respect. In the scriptures, teachings, and practices of the Restoration I find continents waiting to be explored.

If my first self-consciously intellectual engagement with Mormonism began with awareness of the extent to which it presented σκάνδαλον (skandalon), my current faith is defined by a different Greek word: θαυμάζω (thaumazō). Thaumazō can be translated as "wonder." According to Aristotle, all true philosophy begins in thaumazō, a sense of the marvelousness of the universe and the desire to understand it. Before reason or angst there is thaumazō, and it is this that gives rise to intellectual adventure. In light of Aristotle's claim, I find it striking that in the Book of Mormon God refers to the latter-day restoration as "a marvelous work and a wonder." I have a testimony of the truthfulness of the Restoration because of the witness of the Holy Spirit in answer to prayer. I have a testimony because of the blessings that living as a Latter-day Saint has brought into my life and the lives of those that I love. As a scholar, however, I also have a testimony of the Restoration because of the wonder it provokes, and I expect to spend the rest of my life and the life to come learning what it has to teach me.

CHAPTER 3

The Joys and Dangers of a Textual Faith

I confess to a textual faith. I am not proud of this fact. I think that I would be a better disciple if my faith centered more on service to others, personal communion with God, or vanquishing my sins, but the core activity of my spiritual life is reading scripture. I have experienced great joy in this approach. But there are dangers too. Consider Psalm 137:

> By the rivers of Babylon,
> There we sat down,
> Yea, we wept, when we remembered Zion.
> We hanged our harps upon the willows in the midst thereof.
> For there they that carried us away captive required of us a song;
> And they that wasted us required of us mirth,
> Saying, "Sing us one of the songs of Zion."
> How shall we sing the Lord's song in a strange land?
> If I forget thee, O Jerusalem,
> Let my right hand forget her cunning.
> If I do not remember thee,
> Let my tongue cleave to the roof of my mouth;
> If I prefer not Jerusalem above my chief joy.
> Remember, O Lord, the children of Edom
> In the day of Jerusalem;
> Who said, "Rase it, rase it,
> Even to the foundation thereof."
> O daughter of Babylon, who art to be destroyed;
> Happy shall he be, that rewardeth thee
> As thou hast served us.
> Happy shall he be, that taketh and dasheth
> Thy little ones against the stones.

The first three sections of the psalm, verses 1–6, capture beautifully one of the central experiences of being a believer: alienation from the world. In mortality, we find ourselves cast out of Eden, living in Babylon while longing for Jerusalem. We must endure the taunts of those who do not understand the difficulty of singing the Lord's song in a strange land. We pray that we can remember those moments when we have experienced Zion and seek to bind ourselves to them, pledging the cunning of our right hand in the hope of our own faithfulness. In short, reading Psalm

137:1–6 can capture a central spiritual experience and in so doing capture our hearts, giving us tools to sacralize our discomfort with the world.

However, beginning in verse 7, where the psalmist invokes Edom, the experience of reading becomes very different. Now we are to remember the Bronze Age enemies who called for the sacking of Jerusalem. We are not to forget the need for violent retribution against Edom. We must cultivate our thirst for vengeance. The viciousness escalates as the psalm moves to its conclusion, addressing itself to the daughter of Babylon, a mother of young children, and exulting in the brutal murder of her "little ones." As I read the psalm, the bloody schadenfreude of these verses repulses me.

At the beginning of the psalm, I sink uncritically into the language. I let the anguish and longing of the images play across my heart and mind. I insert myself into the scriptural text, and I let that text describe my experience. When I read the end of the psalm, however, I scramble to distance myself from the text. No longer do I read this in terms of some spiritual universal with an authority that applies to me. Rather, my impulse is to historicize, contextualize, and limit the authority of the text. I find no spiritual sustenance in the image of infant brains dashed on rocks, nor do I want anything to do with an authority that would demand such things. Hence, while I am willing to hear the voice of God in verses 1–6, any God who would bless the climax of verses 7–9 would be a monster.

Part of what it means to accept a text as scripture is to accept its authority in the hope that the process of reading scripture has a unique power that other texts lack. Thus, to read a scripture faithfully is to read it hopefully, to read it in the conviction that the act of reading can bring us closer to God. But faithful reading, like all faithful action, comes with challenges—trials and sins that seem to damn our hopes as foolishness. Most Latter-day Saints have little difficulty understanding this dynamic when it is applied to the challenge of following God's commandments in the face of despair and temptation. We would do well to realize that the same is true of the mental activity of faith, perhaps nowhere so much as in reading scripture.

The scriptures contain any number of monstrous passages. Deuteronomy calls for genocide (Deut. 20:17). Revelation delights in images of an orgy of violence against the wicked (Rev. 17). Leviticus decrees the death penalty for gay men (Lev. 20:13). The Book of Mormon contains patently racist verses equating skin color with righteousness (2 Ne. 5:21). What are we to make of such passages? How do we read the scriptures faithfully without succumbing to the darkness toward which these verses seem to call us? Let me suggest two ways of approaching these hard passages. First, we can take them as part of the test of mortality. In Alma 34, Amulek teaches that this life is the time to prepare to meet God, "which is given us to prepare for eternity, behold, if we do not improve our time while in this life, then cometh the night of darkness wherein there can be no labor performed" (v. 32–33). We understand this process of preparation in terms of learning to discern between right and wrong, choosing to follow God, and repenting when we fail to do so. We can read the scriptures in light of this teaching. Consider two passages in the Book of Mormon. One of the hardest verses to read in a world that recognizes the evil of racism is Nephi's account in 2 Nephi 5:21:

> And he [God] had caused the cursing to come upon them, yea, even a sore cursing, because of their iniquity. For behold, they had hardened their hearts against him, that they had become like unto a flint; wherefore, as they were white, and exceedingly fair and delightsome, that they might not be enticing to my people the Lord God did cause a skin of blackness to come upon them.

There are layers of ugliness in this passage. It links righteousness to skin color. It suggests that the Lord uses disgust at miscegenation as a providential tool. It has been the font of much damaging and racist theology. I hate this passage of scripture. I hate reading it. I hated reading it to my children and then laboring with them in the teeth of the text to reject its racist theologizing.

But 2 Nephi 5:21 is not the only thing that the Book of Mormon has to say about race. We can contrast it with the later teachings of Nephi in 2 Nephi 26:33:

> For none of these iniquities come of the Lord; for he doeth that which is good among the children of men; and he doeth nothing save it be plain unto the children of men; and he inviteth them all to come unto him and partake of his goodness; and he denieth none that come unto him, black and white, bond and free, male and female; and he remembereth the heathen; and all are alike unto God, both Jew and Gentile.

In contrast to Nephi's earlier teachings, Nephi here presents a universal view of God's love, one where we are not to impute iniquities to the Lord and where "all are alike unto God." We can understand the process of reading 2 Nephi as presenting us with a choice: will we follow Nephi's earlier teachings, or will we follow his later teachings? They are not consistent with one another. There is a contradiction between the frank conflation of race and righteousness in the earlier passage by Nephi and the universal vision of the later verses.

When we choose Nephi's earlier teachings, we are led toward the world of tribal hatred and human degradation that later passages of the Book of Mormon so graphically illustrate. When we choose to stand with the later verses, we are invited to love those who are different, to seek community as children of God, and to strive to see others in the way that those verses teach us that God sees them. We can deploy the authority of the text for either vision. The scriptures are a challenge to us, inviting us to reveal who we wish to become and how we choose to understand God's purposes.

Second, we can learn from the terrible passages of scripture. As he closes his father's record, Moroni is poignantly aware of the difficult text that he is leaving to us. Directly addressing his readers, he says:

> Condemn me not because of mine imperfection, neither my father, because of his imperfection, neither them who have written before him; but rather give thanks unto God that he hath made manifest unto you our imperfections, that ye may learn to be more wise than we have been (Morm. 9:31).

We often think of wisdom as something that we acquire from reading the scriptures, rather than something that we must bring to them if they are to teach us. Moroni suggests a complex process, one where we are invited to recognize the imperfections in prophets and scripture as a way of being "more wise" than they. This is not a matter of coming to the text as a moral authority trumpeting our superior enlightenment. We become "more wise" through the process of reading itself, of wrestling humbly with the text, and then giving thanks to God for any wisdom received. The emphasis on thanksgiving shifts the source of wisdom from the self to the Lord and dictates the moral and emotional stance we are to take to this process: humility and gratitude rather than pride or self-congratulation.

The danger of fundamentalism in reading scripture does not lie merely in mistaken claims about science or history. Rather, it lies in the mistaken belief that we can accept scripture as a single transparent authority. It pretends that we can follow every teaching and every example in the sacred text and come out the other side with a life both coherent and moral. This is a conceit. It is not true that scripture can be such an authority. A fundamentalist view of scriptural authority is false both because scripture often speaks with conflicting voices—think of the earlier and later teachings of Nephi on race—and because that fundamentalist view fails to recognize the monstrous evil of dashing out the brains of infants on rocks.

But there is a danger, as well, in the kind of reading that I am advocating here. The danger is that we always judge and read scripture based on the beliefs that we bring to it and lose the possibility of scripture confronting and changing our beliefs. A sacred book that does nothing but provide us with an opportunity to glibly issue judgments based on our preexisting beliefs would be of very little value. Such an approach would reduce scripture reading to something more like a political scrum on social media, a kind of vacuous moral preening. Part of the value of a revealed text must be that it challenges our existing beliefs, forces us to reconsider them, and, one hopes, helps us acquire new convictions and commitments that will bring us closer to the Lord.

If we reject the idea that the authority of scripture lies in its status as a complete and consistent encyclopedia of moral and theological teachings, there is also the danger of simply rejecting the authority of scripture. To do this, however, would be to lose the joy and power of a textual faith. Such a faith is based on the hope that through the experience of humbly reading and wrestling with scripture, we experience God and draw closer to him. Like all of mortality, this is a perilous and contingent endeavor, one in which we can give ourselves no assurance of success and can only hope for aid from the Lord and his spirit.

As we struggle toward the light, our only hope lies in a hand that reaches down from above and helps us upward. The text of scripture is a place where that struggle occurs, but what reaches out to us is not the text of scripture but the hand of the living God. The authority of scripture lies in the faith and hope that such an experience can be repeated again and again as we read its pages, including those that we are tempted to pass over.

CHAPTER 4

The Dictation of the Holy Ghost to Us: A Pioneer Day Sermon

Today, I would like to speak about handcart pioneers. In 1855 and 1856 Latter-day Saints across Scandinavia and the British Isles began gathering together their possessions and making their way to North America. They were converts to the church. They had heard the missionaries preach the gospel and the message of the Restoration. They had been touched by the Holy Spirit and had been baptized. They wanted to gather with the Saints. They were looking for a better life for themselves and their families in America, but beyond that they wanted to gather to Zion and assist in the building up of the kingdom of God. Many of them had scrimped and saved for many years to have enough money to make the journey.

They traveled by ship and rail until the railroad ended in Iowa City, Iowa. These Saints were poor, and by the time they arrived in Iowa their money had all but given out. Furthermore, the Church was poor. It lacked the resources to subsidize the purchase of the wagons and ox teams that were usually necessary to cross the interior of the continent. So at the behest of church leaders, these Saints built handcarts and resolved to walk the thousand miles to Utah, pulling their possessions behind them. The first handcart companies to set out left in late spring and early summer. It was a long and exhausting pull, but they arrived safely in the Salt Lake Valley.

The last two companies, however, were delayed and didn't leave Iowa City until early July. It was mid to late August by the time they arrived in Winter Quarters, near present-day Florence, Nebraska.

There they met Levi Savage. Levi Savage was a remarkable man. He had joined the Church and gathered with his family to Nauvoo. There he was a close friend of the Prophet Joseph Smith, and after Joseph's murder Savage went west with the Saints. In 1846, Brigham Young asked him to join the Mormon Battalion, a unit in the US Army, in order to raise money for the rest of the Saints. Levi Savage joined and walked from Florence, Nebraska, all the way to San Diego, California. From there he walked north to San Francisco. From San Francisco he walked across the Sierra Nevadas to rejoin the Saints in the Salt Lake Valley. Brigham Young gave him a few years to catch his breath and then called him on a mission to Siam, in present-day Thailand. It would be difficult to imagine a more remote place for a nineteenth-century American. So Levi Savage walked to San Francisco, then took a ship to Calcutta, India. From there he struggled to make it to Siam, but he was unable to get there due to a civil war. Civil wars were the sort of thing that could finally stop Levi Savage. He did, however, make his way to Rangoon, Burma, in present-day Myanmar and preached the gospel there. At the conclusion of his mission, he boarded a ship sailing west around the Cape of Good Hope to Boston and from thence made his way to Winter Quarters.

Hence, when Levi Savage met up with the Willie Handcart Company he had literally walked or sailed around the entire globe at the behest of church leaders to build up the kingdom of God. He was an experienced frontiersman, someone who knew what was involved in crossing the interior of North America. He begged and pleaded with the European immigrants not to set out so late in the summer. He knew that setting out so late was terribly risky. They could be caught in early winter storms on the high plains, hundreds of miles from their destination. Levi Savage was much more experienced than the leader of the handcart company, James Willie. He seems to have felt threatened by Savage's expertise and his strong opinions. Willie's ego and pride seem to have gotten involved, and he overruled Savage, insisting that the company would leave immediately. At this point, Savage got up and gave a remarkable speech:

> What I have said [about the risks of setting out so late] I know to be true; but seeing you are to go forward, I will go with you, will help all I can, will work with you, will rest with you, and if necessary, will die with you. May God in his mercy bless and preserve us.

Why did Levi Savage go with the handcart pioneers? He didn't have to. He didn't know these people and had never met them before. Their leaders had treated him badly. But they were his people. Their God was his God (Ruth 1:16). They were not strangers or foreigners, but fellow citizens in the household of God (Eph. 2:19). Savage had been baptized and had made covenants that he would bear their burdens that they might be light, would mourn with those of them that mourned, and comfort those that stood by in need of comfort (Mosiah 18:8–9). And he knew that the immigrants would need someone to bear their burdens, to mourn with them, to comfort them.

Savage, of course, was absolutely right. The handcart companies were caught in an early blizzard high on plains of Wyoming more than five hundred miles from their destination. They were unable to move forward, and the members of the company began to die of exhaustion, starvation, exposure, and hypothermia.

Brigham Young learned of the late-departing handcart companies in early October. It was general conference, and the Saints were assembled on Temple Square. Brigham got up and said:

> I will now give this people the subject and the text of the Elders who may speak to-day and during the conference. It is this. On the 5th day of October, 1856, many of our brethren and sisters are on the plains with handcarts, and probably many are now seven hundred miles from this place, and they must be brought here, we must send assistance to them. The text will be, "to get them here." I want the brethren who may speak to understand that their text is the people on the plains. And the subject matter for this community is to send for them and bring them in before winter sets in.
>
> That is my religion; that is the dictation of the Holy Ghost that I possess. It is to save the people. This is the salvation I am now seeking for. . . .
>
> I shall call upon the Bishops this day. I shall not wait until tomorrow, nor until the next day, for 60 good mule teams and 112 or 115 wagons. I do not want to send oxen. I want good horses and mules. They are in this Territory, and we must have them. . . .
>
> I will tell you all that your faith, religion, and profession of religion, will never save one soul of you in the Celestial Kingdom of our God, unless you carry out just such principles as I am now teaching you. Go and bring in those people now on the plains.

Brothers and sisters, suffering seems to be a major part of mortality. Sometimes we suffer because of our own pride and foolishness, like Captain Willie. Sometimes we suffer because of the sin of others. And sometimes we just suffer. Bad things happen to good people, and the Lord doesn't really explain why. He is very clear, however, on what we are supposed to do.

The Savior told a story about a man on the road to Jericho who fell in among thieves (Luke 10:30–37). They beat him, took all of his possessions, and left him for dead in the dirt. A Levite came along. The Levite was a good person. He was keeping all the rules. He no doubt had on a white shirt and tie. But he walked by, leaving the beaten man in the dust. Then along came a Samaritan. I imagine that he was a bit scruffy. He wasn't as good a member of the Church as he could be. He wasn't keeping all of the rules like he should. But he stopped. He bound the man's wounds, picked him up, carried him to an inn, and promised the innkeeper that he would pay for whatever was necessary to heal the man.

Brothers and sisters, we are surrounded by people who are suffering and who face challenges. There are people in our families, in our ward, and in our community who are trapped in the snows high on the plains of Wyoming, who are lying in dust on the road to Jericho. Like Levi Savage, we have covenanted to mourn with them, to help all we can, to work with them. Our job is to go and bring in the people on the plains, to pick them up and carry them to an inn. This is our religion; that is the dictation of the Holy Ghost to us. It is to save the people. This is the salvation that we should seek. I pray that we may do so. In the name of Jesus Christ, amen.

CHAPTER 5

Buying Jewish Whiskey

In a lovely spring garden in suburban Philadelphia, I handed cash and a handkerchief to my friend's rabbi. It was the first time that I, an observant Latter-day Saint, had ever purchased whiskey. For the next two weeks, however, I would own a large store of booze, along with a number of half-used boxes of breakfast cereal, and a lease on a very nice apartment in Jerusalem. At the suggestion of my friend Chaim Saiman, I had agreed to act as a friendly Gentile, purchasing the unused chometz (leavened foodstuffs) and its storage locations that the members of his synagogue were prohibited from owning during Passover. At the conclusion of the holiday, I could, if I so chose, sell the whiskey back to its original owners.

As law professors, Chaim and I share an interest in jurisprudence, law and religion, and contracts. As observant believers, we are both fascinated by the place of religion in the secular world and the way that adherents manage the negotiation between tradition and modernity. The result has been a years-long running conversation on law, contemporary politics, faith and commerce, and—inevitably given Chaim's dual training in yeshiva and law school—halakhah, the vast corpus of Jewish law. When Chaim explained to me that at Passover it was possible to avoid the need to dispose of one's whiskey and other valuable chometz by selling it for the duration of the holiday to a Gentile, I had a new ambition. Legal scholars have long studied how parties use contracts to bargain around troublesome rules. I was fascinated by the idea of contracting around divine law. When I explained to another friend and faculty colleague why I was driving from southern Virginia to Philadelphia in the middle of the week, he said, "Law, religion, and contracts. It's like a religious ritual specifically designed for Nate Oman."

As I understand it, the legal basis for my trip to the Pennsylvania garden begins with Exodus 12, which describes the first Passover and sets forth the rules to be followed thereafter. In verse 15, the text reads "Seven days you shall eat unleavened bread. On the first day you shall remove leaven out of your houses, for if anyone eats what is leavened, from the first day until the seventh day, that person shall be cut off from Israel." The exposition of this rule in Jewish law begins with the earliest halakhic text, the second-century CE compilation known as the Mishnah. The rabbinic debates recorded there explore the contours of the rule in Exodus. To ensure compliance, the house must be scoured for chometz with a candle, and all leavened products burned. To deal with any residual chometz, one must go through the legal ritual of disclaiming ownership, declaring that the chometz is now dust and therefore owned by no one. The debates in the Mishnah were then subject to further commentary and debate in the Talmud. The Talmud in turn has been continuously analyzed and systematized, such as in the Mishneh Torah of Maimonidess, a process that continues unabated to the present. When must the ritual search for chometz begin? What constitutes chometz? (For example, alcohol distilled from grain was brought within the prohibition.) And so on, a thousand debates on each issue over the centuries. As I understand it, the well-established consensus among Orthodox exegetes is that an observant Jew is not allowed to own any chometz during Passover, nor can chometz be stored on the property of a Jew. Centuries ago, however, a problem arose for Jewish distillers. They owned large amounts of chometz, but government regulations made it difficult to simply destroy their stock for Passover. Thus was the workaround of the sale to a friendly Gentile born, a workaround gradually expanded to all of those who wished to avoid burning valuable chometz every spring.

While seemingly baroque to a non-believer, the layering of these rules over the centuries illustrates a basic structure of the religious condition. To be a believer in the modern world is to live in a strange land. It is not that modernity is relentlessly hostile to faith. It is far easier for minority religious communities to live faithfully in contemporary liberal democracies than in any other kind of regime in human history. Our society, however, is not constructed around religious faith. As the Catholic philosopher Charles Taylor has pointed out, secularity isn't so much a society from which faith has been extracted as one in which faith is optional. Within secularity, faith is contingent in a way that it wasn't for previous generations both because of social pressure to religiously conform and because, in a real sense, a life without faith was unthinkable. Most people simply lacked the necessary conceptual machinery to consider a world without the God of their fathers. Secularity is the loss of that sense of necessity and the construction of a social world that aspires to be indifferent to religion. A believer, however, lives in a world where the reality of God continues to sit at the center of existence. The mismatch of the world of belief and the world of secularity constitutes the experience of faith in modernity.

Jewish law provides a marvelous example of this dynamic. Every legal system creates an imaginary world. The common law, for example, imagines a world divided by clear lines of property and planted thick with the obligations of tort and contract. The world in which we actually live never quite corresponds to the law's imagined reality. Legal remedies strive mightily to bring the two into alignment, but good lawyers understand that this effort will always fail in the end. There will always be a gap between legal entitlement and what the legal system can actually deliver as a practical matter. The halakhah is a particularly extreme version of this dynamic. To study the Mishnah and the Talmud is to enter into an at times fantastical jurisprudential world. In this world, the Temple continues to stand in Jerusalem, and pious Jews bring their offerings to the priests to perform the sacrificial rituals. The land is dotted with sanctuary cities and other legal oddities. The Sanhedrin continues to sit and the intricacies of its procedures mete out justice to Israel. All of these laws continue to be studied in exhaustive detail in modern yeshivas.

To call the world of Jewish law imaginary or fantastical is not, I hope, to insult or belittle it in any way. It is only to point out the way that the halakhah creates an entire world whose existence would be unguessed at by a foreigner to the legal texts. However, after a lifetime of devotional Talmud study, it is a world that lawyers and hedge fund managers in suburban Philadelphia, members in good standing of America's technocratic elite, can enter with ease.

The life of Orthodox Judaism in part seems to be an effort to inhabit the world of halakhah in the face of a social world that is very different from the one envisioned by the law. Part of how one does this is simply by studying, discussing, and debating the law. Indeed there is a real sense in which much of the halakhah exists in order to be studied. For anyone who has even a passing familiarity with a functioning legal system, it is clear that much of Jewish law exists as a vehicle for jurisprudential discussion rather than as a system of operative rules. But the halakhic world isn't inhabited purely through classroom debate. One also enters that world by following those rules of Jewish law that have been blessed by tradition and experience with concrete practical significance. Indeed, as I understand it, much of the work of response and commentary over the two millennia since the Mishnah was first written has been an effort to mediate and manage the tension of living in both the concrete world of any particular historical moment and the world of halakhah simultaneously. In other words, halakhah as a living practice is a way of being a Jew in a world where being Jewish is optional. There is thus a sense in which Orthodox Judaism, far from being an insular or reactionary retreat from secularity, represents a kind of virtuoso performance of faith in a secular world. Indeed, Jews have been living in a secular world, in Taylor's sense, for far longer than Christians. They are better at it. They have more experience.

I think that this kind of performance is on display in the effort to bargain around God's law. There is a temptation for both believers and critics to imagine faithfulness in fundamentalist terms. There is some pristine original template for living the faithful life, and "real" religion consists of unbending adherence to its strictures. Such fundamentalism, however, is an illusion. The pristine template never actually existed; it is always a past constructed after the fact with the troublesome bits excised from memory. More importantly, fidelity is always dynamic, a matter of managing allegiance to an evolving tradition that is continually both resisting and accommodating the world. Even those who purport to be following a fundamentalist path are doing this. The question for a believer is thus always how one adapts a tradition while accepting its authority and maintaining fidelity to it.

One can think about this question by analogy to the process of legal change. The great nineteenth-century jurist and historian Henry Sumner Maine claimed that legal systems change in one of three ways: by legislation, by equity, and by fiction. Legislation is an idea familiar to laypersons, but equity and fiction in the legal context have specific meanings. Equity refers to a loose interpretation of a rule in order to achieve substantial justice. Fiction refers to the process of adapting legal rules by agreeing to pretend that their conditions have been met when in fact they have not. Good Victorian that he was, Maine thought in terms of progress, with fiction being the most primitive form of legal change and legislation representing the most advanced stage. Like most Victorian narratives of progress, this one doesn't hold up terribly well to scrutiny, but Maine was on to something in his taxonomy. These are, in fact, the ways in which legal systems change in practice. Applied to divine law, however, the tool kit can become fraught.

Christians are generally fond of equity. They purport to look beyond the surface of rules to see their inner spirit, a spirit that can be applied with considerable flexibility. Hence, Christians read the Hebrew Bible through the lens of Paul's hyper-abstraction in which the true "spirit" of the rule can be its negation. To take an extreme example, Paul argues in his epistles that the true spirit of circumcision consists in not being circumcised. This allows for flexibility, to be sure, but one can understand the skepticism of a Jewish reader as to whether Paul is in fact being true to the law revealed on

Sinai. Indeed, one of the vices of Christian spirituality is its tendency to abstract from tradition. All historical contingency falls away in the search for a transcendent and universal spirit. This creates a constant risk of self-negation. I suspect that this is especially true for the kind of Evangelical Protestantism that dominates much of American Christianity. Essentially Calvinist in its theology, American Evangelicalism often emphasizes spirit over law and the personal, subjective experience of being saved over the demands of liturgy or strict behavioral codes. This subjective focus can risk a drift toward a stance of "spiritual but not religious." A certain numinous psychology can replace theology, and the language of therapy and self-help can eclipse the drama of sin and repentance.

Mormonism presents a similar danger of self-negation, but it does so through religious legislation rather than equity. Latter-day Saints are marked as heretics from Christian orthodoxy in part by their belief in living prophets and continuing revelation. The idea of a hierarchy that can speak with God and speak for God opens up the possibility of religious legislation in a way that doesn't exist, I suspect, for most Christians and Jews. To be sure, the hierarchy's claims to such expansive authority risks abuse, and a god who replaces one revealed law with another revealed law may be puzzling. If one risks the paradox of an eternal God whose demands can change, however, the mechanics of religious accommodation, even religious revolution, become easier.

The approach taken by my tradition has its own risks and pitfalls. On one hand, it can tend toward a dysfunctionally expansive fundamentalism in which every statement of the ecclesiastical hierarchy or institutional church becomes freighted with the authority of divine revelation. The result is a belief that would seem to promise an unusually dynamic form of religion can, in practice, become rigidly conservative and sclerotic. Ironically, however, an opposite danger also exists. Continuing revelation locates the present between a past filled with revelations that have been superseded and a future filled with revelations that have yet to be given. This creates a dynamic that has a tendency to dissolve all religious claims in the present, particularly religious claims embedded with the concrete experience of the Latter-day Saints themselves. Thus what begins as an apparently extreme claim to authority can ironically turn on itself with the authority of the future claimed against the authority of the present by invoking the example of the past.

Armed with an appreciation for the dangers of equity and legislation, legal fiction looks more attractive. The rabbi to whom I conveyed the cash in exchange for the chometz insisted on the juridical reality of our transactions. The moment was embedded in a series of legal formalities designed to emphasize the complete transfer of the chometz to my ownership. I was assured that I had every right to take and consume the whiskey if I wished to do so. He made it clear, for example, that I had the right to enter the Jewish homes whose pantries I had leased and make off with my Cheerios and booze. The exchange was structured as both a cash sale and a bartered exchange (handkerchief for whiskey) to eliminate any difficulties under Jewish law as to my ownership. It turns out there is some doubt as to how to make a binding contract with a Gentile, and the redundant contractual structures were a response to that ambiguity.

I was also told that for the transactions to be valid as a matter of halakhah, it must also be valid under the governing non-Jewish law. Accordingly, I signed a document that purported to be a sale of goods under Pennsylvania law. On this latter point, I will admit to some skepticism. Despite Chaim's diligent lawyering, title to the chometz may have remained with the original owners under Pennsylvania law. Our mutual understanding of the deal looked much more like a lease or a secured loan than a sale. While we were careful not to say so, it was understood by all present that I would be selling the chometz back at the end of Passover. There is a long legal tradition of using dummy sales for transactional purposes other than the transfer of property. Perhaps I was really just renting the chometz for a short period or, alternatively, making a small cash loan with future advances secured by the chometz as collateral. Both are real possibilities under American commercial law, which tends to treat transactions according to their economic reality rather than according to the labels that parties give them. This is a potential problem, as with both a lease and a secured loan my Jewish friends would retain title to their chometz during Passover.

To be sure, there are enough doctrinal complications in the contract Chaim drafted that it might survive the acid wash of the Uniform Commercial Code's functionalism. In contract law, the parole evidence rule, which sharply limits the evidence that courts may consider in contract cases, can cover a multitude of sins. Certainly, one could argue in good faith that the contract has enough validity under the secular law to be valid under Jewish law. Still, the entire transaction had more than a whiff of the legal fiction about it, a mass of formality designed to say that we are doing one thing while actually doing something very different. In my mind, it is the double-mindedness of the legal fiction that is brilliant. Sitting in the suburban garden in Philadelphia, it was impossible not to feel the authority of Jewish law. Indeed, several members of the synagogue were there to witness the transaction with their children for precisely that reason. The forms and signatures literally had no other purpose than to comply with the demands laid down in Exodus. The dynamics of equity and legislation that tend to erase the very traditions from which they spring were wholly absent from the transaction. If anything, the very particularity of the legal formalities mitigated against the Christian danger of dissolving religion into spirituality. Legal formalities work precisely because they are strange and serve no purpose outside of the law. The purpose of a formality is to clearly differentiate to participants between actions that have a legal significance and those that do not. No one, for example, accidentally files a real estate deed in their local circuit court without understanding that they are performing a legal act. There is always a risk, however, of legal formalities becoming too familiar. As a legal formality becomes widely used outside of the legal context, it decays, losing the ability to differentiate between legally significant action and legally irrelevant action. In order to work, a formality must be weird. When the law at issue is divine, properly functioning legal formalities will be oddities that make it impossible to forget the claims of God. They are ritual acts that exist only to comply with divine law. At the same time, there is a sense in which the entire transaction selling the chometz existed to avoid the harsh requirements of that law. The continuity of the suburban whiskey collections were maintained. The fiction manages the problems of fidelity and evolution, allowing the tradition to change without negating itself.

There are, of course, limits to bargaining around God's commands. A law that collapses completely into fiction is terminally ill, but judiciously used legal fictions create a suppleness that allows one to bend without breaking, change without forgetting. This is precisely the challenge of secularity. A world in which religion is optional is one in which it can be forgotten. The threat to religious survival in secularity is less the polemics of the irreligious than the indifference of those who have forgotten how to be religious.

The danger of Christian or Mormon strategies of evolution is that they lend themselves to forgetting. Protestant Christianity can exalt a subjective encounter with the spirit in a way that can all too easily dissolve into subjectivism. The idea of continuing revelation, on the other hand, tends to render every Latter-day Saint claim to authority contingent, gnawing away at its own foundations in a way that risks the collapse of the entire tradition. There are virtues to ritual, formality, and fiction that both traditions would be wise to find ways of cultivating. The very oddity of selling Jewish whiskey to a Latter-day Saint makes the forgetting of tradition impossible. It's part of the genius for change without forgetting that has made the survival of Judaism possible in a world that for Jews has been secular since at least the destruction of the Second Temple in 70 CE. A healthy respect for and fascination with that success, along with my friendship with Chaim, led me to the garden in Pennsylvania and will, I hope, lead me to buy more Jewish whiskey in Passovers to come.

Next year in Philadelphia!

INTELLECT

CHAPTER 6

The Disposition of Mormonism

Introduction

This essay offers an argument about what we can call the dispositional tendency of Mormonism. My argument is that Latter-day Saint teachings incline one to a conservative stance toward the world, or at least toward religious faith. This is a claim about dispositions, not political ideology. A disposition consists of the unstated prejudices that exist before ideology, the basic instincts that we use to make sense of the world. Broadly speaking, there are three dispositions at work in modern Western societies. To oversimplify in the interests of conversation, there is a conservative disposition that sees the world through the lens of gratitude, a liberal disposition that sees the world through the lens of choice, and a progressive disposition that sees the world through the lens of liberation. Because dispositions consist of habits and prejudices, not intellectual systems, no person's disposition consists solely of one of these approaches in any pure and consistent way. Accordingly, in this essay dispositions are offered as a kind of ideal type for our habits and prejudices.

In support of my claim that Mormonism inclines toward a conservative disposition, I will offer an analysis of the Latter-day Saint concept of God and the Latter-day Saint reading of the Fall and of God's covenant with Israel. These subjects are chosen because they are striking and suggestive, though they cannot, taken together, be said to constitute even the whole of Latter-day Saint theology, let alone Mormon history and practice, all of which participate in the making of a disposition. Hence, the argument here can only be suggestive and not demonstrative. Furthermore, it must be remembered that Mormonism will be but one input, and often not the most important input, of any individual Latter-day Saint's disposition. This is not an essay in psychology or political science, but an attempt, however limited, to get at some of the deep intellectual tendencies of Latter-day Saint thought.

We all have a basic orientation or disposition. We might think of a disposition as our basic set of assumptions about the world. These assumptions aren't simply intellectual or even primarily intellectual. They are also emotional, spiritual, and even aesthetic. Our disposition is the sum total of our prejudices. By prejudices, I don't mean a set of irrational and odious beliefs. Rather, I am using the term more literally. The root of prejudice is the Latin word "iudicere," meaning "to judge," to which a prefix is attached. A prejudice is thus that which comes before judgment. Our prejudices are the framework that makes judgment possible. This does not mean that they cannot be examined or reconsidered. Rather, my claim is that there is no point at which we begin thinking without our prejudices. They always orient us.

This is an essay about dispositions. My argument is that Latter-day Saint theology pushes toward a conservative disposition. Another way of putting this point is that Mormonism has a set of conservative prejudices. It might be possible to construct a more elaborate political theology based on Latter-day Saint doctrines, but I am skeptical of the value of such projects. Hence, my project here is more modest. At the same time, it is potentially more ambitious if, as I suggest, our dispositions and prejudices necessarily structure our thinking, providing a shape to our thoughts prior to any explicit reflection. It also implies that Mormonism will necessarily sit uneasily with rival dispositions, in particular those I shall call liberal or progressive.

A Conservative Disposition

What do I mean by a conservative disposition? At the heart of the conservative disposition is the sense that one has received something precious from the past that ought to be protected from destruction. Conservatives are distrustful of violent change. Chief among those precious inheritances are the communities in which we find ourselves. Families, neighborhoods, and nations are all precious. A distrust of change does not presuppose hostility to all change. A conservative disposition, however, prefers incremental and marginal change to wholesale or revolutionary change. The evolutionary and the organic is better than the rationalized and the novel. Communities are not simply something precious to be preserved; communities constitute us—we are never really independent individuals. We cannot be who we are without our histories and our communities. We identify with others, not simply because of sympathy but because they are part of a "we," a "we" without which "I" cannot exist. This creates a certain vulnerability. Attacks on communities can be attacks on our identity. It also creates a certain robustness of the self. To see one's identity as tied up with a rooted community is to be rooted oneself. To know where you come from is to know who you are, and that knowledge renders the self less exposed to corrosive anxieties over identity and place in the world. Coupled together, the conservation of that which is precious and the intertwining of identity and community yields a disposition toward time and persons. Key to the conservative disposition are ideas of forebearers and descendants. At the most primal level, this is literal and genetic. We are a balance between past and future. In a sense, we are a conduit by which gifts pass from grandmothers and grandfathers to granddaughters and grandsons. This sense of forming a connection between the past and the future, however, extends beyond kin and family. Although family and kin occupy a special place in the conservative disposition, those precious things that we have, whether they be traditions, communities, institutions, nature, or material prosperity, are bequeathed to us from the past. We enjoy far more than we could create for ourselves, and that which we enjoy is the laborious creation of previous ages, easily destroyed. It is to be conserved, not simply to be consumed and enjoyed, but to be passed on to those who follow us.

Finally, the thickly embedded self of the conservative has a particular disposition toward authority in its most primal sense. Authority is something that arises outside of the self. It arrives from someplace else and makes demands on us, disciplining our lives. We owe debts to the past, to the future, and to our communities. These debts are not self-imposed. Rather, we inherit them at birth and carry them throughout our lives. They are never fully discharged. The weight of these debts is not a form of tyranny or oppression. Rather, they arise from the nature of human life itself. To be a person is to be subject to the claims of authority. We are not naturally free, if by free we mean the absence of duties and obligations.

A Liberal Disposition

The content of a conservative disposition can be illuminated by contrasting it with what we might call a liberal disposition. The liberal disposition begins with free individualism. Everything follows from the prejudice that what is good in life is for the individual to own himself and to chart his own destiny. Where the conservative sees the world first as containing precious inheritances to be saved, the liberal looks out on a world filled with choices, and he experiences himself as possessed of the power to pursue those choices. To inherit something is to receive a gift, but it is a gift that one cannot reject without a certain violence. The conservative is thus in possession of certain precious things, but they also weigh upon him. In the liberal ideal, we possess only what we choose to possess, and its value to the individual arises precisely because it is chosen. The liberal appreciates community, but the communities that most appeal to the liberal imagination are those that are intentional and chosen. Ideally, we choose our communities rather than being born into them or thrown into them by other accidents beyond our control.

The liberal disposition therefore reverses the relationship between individual and community from that in the conservative disposition. For the conservative, individual identity takes its shape and content in large part from communities. As Aristotle suggested, we are constituted by our polis. In contrast, the liberal insists that, properly speaking, the individual is primal and communities are constituted by the choice and deliberation of their members. For the liberal disposition, consent is the ultimate source of authority and obligation. Philosophically, this manifests itself in social contract theories that seek to explain the claims of community in terms of some original agreement. It is also manifested in what can be called philosophical contractarianism, in which one discovers the scope of all moral obligations by imagining what rules of conduct would command the universal consent of free and rational individuals. In effect, contractarianism expands the social contract argument to include not just political authority but all forms of ethical obligation.

The emphasis on the choice of free individuals also yields a different attitude toward persons and time. The prototypical form of human obligation is contractual. We owe to others an obligation not to interfere in the scope of their ability to choose. But our obligations do not arise out of our membership in unchosen communities. Certainly, one's forebearers impose no obligations. We cannot be said to be responsible for or to anyone based on actions taken by others before we were born. We may have obligations to the unborn, but only the obligation not to undermine their choices. The liberal disposition, however, doesn't feel obligation to descendants because they are ours, an extension of the unchosen web of community that defines our identity.

Finally, liberalism has difficulties with the idea of authority. Social contract stories seek to justify a spare form of political authority. The assumption of such stories, however, is that authority is presumptively illegitimate. To be morally permissible, authority must always be generated from within the individual. Behavior that is self-regarding or, in the more contemporary formulation, behavior that is not related to maintaining the conditions of meaningful individual choice, is beyond the reach of any moral evaluation or disapprobation. Where a conservative disposition sees authority as a claim from beyond the self that disciplines choice, for the liberal, claims to authority unrooted in the self and its choices are the *sine qua non* of illegitimate oppression.

A Progressive Disposition

What we might call a progressive disposition consists in the exaggeration of liberal tropes. At the heart of this disposition lies the hope of liberation. Liberalism grounds communities and obligations in the choosing, contracting self. The liberal is thus quite optimistic about the self and its capacities. The liberal disposition finds it easy to believe in the existence of a self with desires and plans worthy of respect. Likewise, the liberal self is assumed to have the ability to choose in meaningful ways among plans and desires. The progressive disposition shares the liberal assumption about the priority of freedom and choice, but it is haunted by anxieties about the capacities of the self. One way to think about the progressive disposition is that it has liberal dreams but conservative nightmares. Where the conservative disposition sees in the situated self a source of meaning, identity, and authority, the progressive disposition sees oppression so long as the communities fail—as actual communities always do—to instantiate a just society. The embeddedness of the self is particularly insidious because it suggests that our ideas and desires, the apparent grounds of personal autonomy, are in fact infected with odious injustices. Likewise, our apparently free choices result from accidents of birth and history that may be dictated by the happenstance of past and present evils. At the very moment when the liberal feels greatest ease, freely choosing to act in accordance with self-formulated plans, the progressive feels anxiety and fears the legacy of oppression.

The liberal disposition can take a moderate attitude toward time. To be sure, the liberal disposition sees progress from an illiberal past, but he can imagine a future in which we live freely in consensual communities. For a progressive, history has a stronger sense of motion. The past is an oppressed country, and tradition is likely simply the agent of oppression invading the present. Because true freedom requires not just consent but a just society in which the choices of the socially constituted self can be respected free of anxiety, the work of liberation is never complete. There are always new fronts in the battle for freedom and justice, because the mere absence of coercion is insufficient to vouchsafe liberation. Taken to extremes, the progressive disposition may be drawn to radical or even violent political utopianism, but like any other disposition, progressivism is seldom taken to its logical conclusion.

A progressive disposition can also manifest itself as constant skepticism about, and opposition to, the received structures of oppression. While a progressive disposition need not become utopian, the ethos of constantly striving for the always receding promise of a better world generates a distinctive stance toward authority. First, the idea of traditional or communal authority becomes incomprehensible or pernicious. Indeed, such a notion of authority is one of the chief evils against which the progressive feels called to struggle. This does not mean, however, that the progressive accepts the liberal idea of authority arising from consent. There are too many ways in which history and society can taint consent. Rather, authority rises from the process of liberation itself. Those battling on the frontier between liberation and oppression can claim authority because only in the struggle of liberation can the anxieties of omniscient oppression be muted.

These sketches are simplified and overdrawn. I have called them dispositions, but they aren't accounts of human psychology. Rather, they lay out common sets of assumptions about how one might approach the world, especially the social and political world. This is not to say that everyone would articulate their assumptions in this way, or that those with what I am calling conservative, liberal, or progressive dispositions couldn't articulate them in different ways. Likewise, actual character and belief are complicated. We are seldom, perhaps never, wholly one thing or another. We are likely to have intuitions and impulses that could take root in multiple dispositions. There is no *a priori* reason that our assumptions and prejudices are consistent and coherent. Indeed, it would be surprising if they were.

All these caveats aside, however, I think that many—perhaps most—people in modern societies gravitate more toward one or two of these dispositions. Hopefully, they seem familiar to the reader, and she recognizes them in herself and in those she knows. Their value lies not in their ability to describe the beliefs of particular individuals, but in their ability to render explicit what is often implicit, and thereby form a starting point for examining our beliefs and actions.

Restoration and Revelation

Mormonism begins with revelation. In the early 1830s in Kirtland, Ohio, Joseph Smith and his associates established a School of the Prophets. The name was taken from the Bible, and its purpose was to instruct new converts not only in theology but in secular subjects as well. The project produced the *Lectures on Faith*,[1] which provided a systematic exposition of Latter-day Saint principles, beginning with the nature of God. Today, the *Lectures on Faith* are little read by Latter-day Saints, much of their theology having been superseded by Joseph Smith's subsequent revelations. They do, however, contain a striking passage that illustrates the way in which the Latter-day Saint emphasis on revelation shapes one's approach to God and the world. The *Lectures* begin with a chapter on the nature of belief, followed by a chapter on the character of God. Each chapter ends with "Questions and answers on the foregoing principles." To the question "How did men first come to a knowledge of the existence of God so as to exercise faith in him?" the text responds with the biblical story of Adam and Eve in the Garden conversing with God, their Fall and expulsion from Eden, and God's further conversations with them in the lone and dreary world. The resort to the Genesis narrative is unsurprising for authors writing in the biblically soaked culture of religious enthusiasts in 1830s America. Furthermore, the questions and answers in the *Lectures* seem to have been designed to provide prospective Latter-day Saint missionaries with proof texts from the Bible to be used in the public debates that formed such a central part of nineteenth-century Latter-day Saint proselytizing. Interestingly, in the passage that follows the questions and their accompanying scriptural stories, the book states, "What is the object of the foregoing? It is that it may be clearly seen how it was that the first thoughts were suggested to the minds of men of the existence of God, and how extensively this knowledge was spread among the immediate descendants of Adam."

To see the import of this passage, compare it to the argument made by Rene Descartes in *The Discourse on Method*. Descartes's ambition in that work is to provide a sure foundation for knowledge by subjecting all

1. The authorship of the *Lectures on Faith* has been the subject of a lively scholarly discussion. Traditionally, Latter-day Saints have assumed that Joseph Smith authored the lectures, but modern scholars argue that they were in whole or in part written by Sidney Rigdon. Until the early twentieth century, they were printed in the Doctrine and Covenants and accepted as one of the standard works of the Church.

his beliefs and perceptions to the acids of systematic doubt. Eventually, he falls back on the famous "cogito ergo sum," the undoubtable proposition that "I think, therefore I am." Having escaped utter skepticism, however, Descartes still feels himself trapped in a position where even the basic data of sense perception must be dismissed as unreliable. Descartes finds his escape in God. Looking within his mind, he finds there the concept of God as an inherent part of his mental architecture. From this concept, he proceeds via a variation on Anselm's ontological argument to the conclusion that God exists and that He would not permit us to be systematically mistaken. Notice that in Descartes's argument, the concept of God is a basic feature of the individual mind, and that mind is automatically equipped with the resources to generate a proof for God's existence, unaided by anything else. For Descartes, religious belief is thus a sort of implication of his own intellectual self-sufficiency. For the *Lectures on Faith*, in contrast, religious belief is a gift. There is no suggestion that unaided human reason will arrive at a proof and belief in God. Indeed, even the first thought that there might be a being such as God comes because He reveals himself. Mormonism rejects the notion of God as a metaphysical origin for existence. Rather, He organizes matter unorganized and inhabits a universe filled with coeternal intelligences who can neither be created nor destroyed. This vision of a God that exists within a metaphysical frame, rather than outside of it, has implications for Latter-day Saint spirituality. First, it forms the basis for a personal relationship with God, one that promises not simply a subjective experience with a transcendent divine but what Joseph Smith called "sociality." Like Adam, we can hope to walk with God through the Garden in the cool of the evening.

Alfred North Whitehead observed that "[t]he God of the philosophers is not available for religious purposes." The God of Mormonism, however, emphatically *is* available. Indeed, in the view of some critics, He is too available, and a deity shorn of metaphysical transcendence ceases to be an object worthy of religious devotion. An implication of the finitistic God of Mormonism is that His existence is not a necessary truth. God is a being that happens to exist and might conceptually not exist. This doesn't mean that one believes that human reason is unable to formulate arguments for God's existence. Latter-day Saint finitism isn't a form of fideism, declaring belief in the absence of any justification for belief. With Peter, Latter-day Saints are ready "always to give an answer to every man that asketh the reason for the hope that is in [them]" (1 Pet. 3:15). The answer they give, however, does not lie in a deduction from the nature of their own intellectual existence. Rather, Latter-day Saint answers are always contingent, and ultimately, they are contingent on God's revelation of Himself. If the *Lectures on Faith* are to be believed, the very availability of a concept of God rests on a primal theophany.

Thus for a Latter-day Saint, knowledge of God is a gift in at least two senses. First, it is a gift from God in the first instance because it is only by his revelation of Himself that it is available. It is a divine gift, rather than the achievement of individuals reasoning from first premises. Second, it is a gift because the knowledge of past revelations is dependent on a chain of transmission, with each generation passing on to its children knowledge inherited from ancestors. There is also gratitude for the gift of new revelations as the stories change over time, reinterpreted to give meaning in new circumstances. The process of change and evolution, however, is never the individual creation or discovery of something new. Rather, it is a process of adapting an inheritance that is always a gift from the past to be preserved and passed on to the future. Coupled with the idea of revelation are the concepts of apostasy and restoration. The primal revelation of Mormonism to Joseph Smith was ultimately the recovery of something precious that was lost. This is true despite the way in which the devotional account of Latter-day Saint origins has shifted over time. Today, Latter-day Saints tell the story by beginning with the First Vision, a narrative in which God announces a general apostasy and calls on Joseph Smith to be His instrument of restoration. The emphasis on the First Vision, however, is a twentieth-century practice. Earlier Latter-day Saints began their story with the coming forth of the Book of Mormon, a forgotten scripture speaking from the dust. Both origin stories hinge on the recovery of what was lost or corrupted.

Joseph Smith spoke of Mormonism as a force to revolutionize the world. Speaking in the generations after the French Revolution, "revolutionize" could mean something like violent and radical change. It thus seems like a liberal or progressive gesture. However, there is an older meaning of the word revolution that is perhaps more apt. As Hannah Arendt has pointed out, revolution literally meant a turn, as in the revolution of a wheel on its axle or the globe on its axis. A revolution thus noted a massive change, but one that involved a return back to something that was lost. Hence, for example, the seventeenth-century theorists of English revolution conceptualized the struggle against royal absolutism not in terms of the abstract rights of man but as a recovery of the lost privileges of Englishmen. So important was the narrative of a revolutionary turning to the past that when the actual English past failed to provide the precedents required by the present, they felt called upon to invent them.

This older meaning of revolution seems to rest most easily within Mormonism. In Joseph Smith's revelations, the familiar story of progression from the Old Testament to the New Testament is replaced with a cyclical story of dispensations. We learn in the Book of Moses that the whole of Christ's gospel was revealed to Adam and subsequent premeridian prophets as humanity lost or corrupted what had been previously revealed. Hence, the text of the law revealed on Sinai was supplemented by additional revelations not recorded in the canonical scriptures. The supplemental revelation, however, was not the Oral Law of the Talmud, but rather the Christian gospel in its native purity, a gospel that, because of subsequent disbelief and apostasy, was lost. To be sure, at times Smith spoke of mysteries to be revealed that had been hidden from the foundations of the world. But far more commonly, he presented revelation as the recovery of a lost past, whether in the form of golden plates, Egyptian papyri, or even in some cases, ancient texts revealed without the physicality of any ancient objects.

Even the discontinuity between apostasy and restoration can be overstated. For all of the rather pointless wrangling over whether Latter-day Saints are "really Christian," Smith and his revelations unquestionably operate within the Christian tradition. Mormonism is very far from being entirely the creation of revelations restoring lost materials. Most strikingly, it is utterly dependent on the Bible, whose stories it integrates, interprets, and reinterprets. Nor is the Bible its only point of continuity with the Christian tradition. While largely devoid of formally trained theologians or even thinkers that are fully conscious of their intellectual debts, the Latter-day Saints have defined themselves in large part using concepts from the Christian theological tradition, even as they have adopted and changed those concepts, often in the give and take of religious polemic. Likewise, scholars have noted that the ecclesiological language of Joseph Smith's early revelations assume continuity with the Christian tradition.[2] Contemporary Latter-day Saints assume that when Smith's revelations speak of "the church," they refer specifically to The Church of Jesus Christ of Latter-day Saints. In Smith's early revelations, however, the Lord speaks of "my church" as an already existing body before the formal creation of the Church of Christ on April 6, 1830. In other words, the

2. Terryl Givens and Fiona Givens deserve credit for this insight.

revelations used the term "church" to refer to the whole body of Christian believers, rather than to any particular institution. This usage is foreign to contemporary Latter-day Saints, but is a well-accepted part of traditional Christian discourse, one that emphasizes the continuity of Christian practices and communities.

Latter-day Saint writers have a tendency to talk about the Restoration and the founding revelations of Mormonism in terms that emphasize their novelty, their radicalism, and their discontinuity with the past. In part this is just good history. Early Latter-day Saints often came from the ideological fringes of sectarian Protestantism, and they were likely to be people disenchanted with their religious heritage. They were seeking "the gifts of the spirit"—new, individual religious experiences. It is also precisely the anxiety sparked by the Restoration's continuity with the past that often leads Latter-day Saints to emphasize the novelty of Mormon revelations. Only if the Restoration is new can its claims to divine authority be maintained.

Finally, Latter-day Saints of a progressive or liberal disposition are fond of casting the Restoration in more contemporary revolutionary terms because they have a natural prejudice against continuity and the past. Joseph Smith's teachings are appealing as much for their iconoclasm as for any ideas he produced. Progress requires iconoclasts fearlessly breaking with the past, and to cast Joseph Smith and the Restoration in these terms gives one's religion a certain progressive respectability. This need for ideological respectability is perhaps most acute for progressive Church members in the United States, where contemporary Latter-day Saints are most likely to be found involved in center-right or right-wing politics.

There is a sense, however, in which such academic, apologetic, liberal, and progressive reactions are external to Mormonism. This doesn't mean that they are mistaken or inauthentic, only that they are missing something important. The historian sits on an academic perch and pokes at and opines on Mormonism as a social phenomenon, but academics—as academics—do not inhabit the cosmos that Mormonism creates.[3] An apologetic stance also fails, perhaps ironically, to fully enter into the Latter-day Saint world. The apologist stands at the borders of the kingdom, defending it against a hostile world. He faces out, operating in a world where the

---

3. I don't mean to imply that historians of Mormonism cannot be faithful Latter-day Saints. Many of them are. Rather, my claim is merely that the academic discourse of history never enters fully into the intellectual world of Mormonism. To do so would be to forfeit its claim of being academic discourse.

truth claims of the Restoration are under constant pressure and must be defended to the critic or the doubter. Like the historian, he is doing necessary and honorable work. However, apologetics by definition must treat the object of its apology as up for grabs, and thus never has the luxury of simply accepting the faith and working out its meaning. The progressive reading of the Restoration as an iconoclastic revolution enters into Mormonism but does so only shallowly. It sees the important fact as being that Joseph Smith and the Restoration are a break with their surrounding culture and history. The emphasis on the break, however, is driven mainly by the need to assuage progressive anxieties. The anxiety isn't social.[4] Rather, it flows from the sense that to be truly right and good, something must be progressive, an agent in the struggle for liberation. If one has a progressive disposition and one loves and values one's Mormonism, it is natural that one should cast it in progressive terms. The shallowness of the reading is ultimately a gesture of love and faith.[5] If one fully enters into the Latter-day Saint cosmos, however, Joseph Smith is not an iconoclast, and the Restoration is not a break from the past. Rather, they recapitulate a tradition that goes back to Adam. It is a tradition in which divine knowledge is a gift, rather than an individual intellectual achievement. Our role is to treasure this gift, protect it, and deliver it intact to the next generation. The only revolution is the return of lost things, the recovery of ancient wisdom. This is not a message of liberal self-sufficiency or progressive struggle toward liberation. Rather, it is a story of conservation and recovery, a story of redemptive conservatism.

It is, however, a cosmic story, and one might therefore point out that it lacks an attachment to a locality, or an actually existing tradition. This is a fair point. What is striking about Joseph Smith and the early Latter-day Saints is how rapidly they sought to attach this cosmic story to a particular

---

4. Although it may be. Fitting in as a Latter-day Saint and therefore a presumed reactionary in a progressive social milieu is not always easy, as I can attest from a professional lifetime in such spaces. It's natural to use all the rhetorical resources at one's disposal.

5. One might also point out that it is also, for that reason, incoherent in some sense. To love Mormonism as a tradition is ultimately a conservative rather than a progressive gesture, even when the reasons for the love of the tradition are cashed out in progressive terms. This incoherence isn't necessarily a vice, of course, as any individual disposition will contain competing and inconsistent impulses. It is ironic, however, and a testament to the allure of conservatism as much as of progressivism.

place and make it the story of a particular people. Latter-day Saints gathered to build Zion. In gathering, they made themselves a people, and the cosmic story of dispensations and restorations became their story, an ancient tradition provided for a new people. Likewise, the ambition of Latter-day Saint missionaries is never simply an individual conversion. Rather, ideally, every convert baptism leads to the temple and the foundation of a new Latter-day Saint family redeeming its dead and passing the gospel to its children. Strikingly, while the language of novelty and revolution has wide currency among Latter-day Saint intellectuals, historians, apologists, and progressives, in the vernacular of Church teachings and practices, we nest the Latter-day Saint past in the language of divine patterns and gratitude. Modern Saints follow in the footsteps of God's people throughout history, and the founding generations of Mormonism are more likely to be honored as the testators of a precious inheritance than as revolutionaries whose iconoclasm is to be emulated. A similar tendency toward a conservative disposition can be discerned in Latter-day Saint stories of the Fall and in ideas of covenant.

Social Contracts

In the beginning, man lived in the state of nature. Thus far, the stories of Genesis and social contract theories track one another. Both appeal to a primal era. In this primeval state, humanity lived differently than they do today, somehow more naturally. One imagines that both Eden and Locke's state of nature contained few cities and a great deal of foliage. They both imagine humanity operating in a normative universe quite different than the one we inhabit today. The stories are meant to explain how we got from there to here, and in doing so, they promise to reveal the deep structure of our obligations and rights. Thus far, they are the same. From this point forward, however, they diverge. For the contract stories of Hobbes and Locke, life in the Garden is poor, nasty, brutish, and short, although the Hobbesian Garden is much more brutish than the Lockean one. Both of them see the pre-normative state of nature as a place of endemic conflict with no central authority to promulgate laws and see to their enforcement. Humanity is left to its worst angels. Again, Hobbes presents a more violent and anomic world than Locke—the English Civil War having been a bloodier affair than the Glorious Revolution—but both assume that social obligations and institutions to enforce them are necessary to escape the violence and potential chaos of the Garden. Ultimately, they conclude that individuals in the state of nature would agree to a set of rules and institutions limiting predation and securing peace and protection. Hence, by contract, humanity leaves the Garden and creates society.

The English social contract theorists take it as axiomatic that if we can show that the origins of social institutions lie in agreement, then the institutions are legitimate. Indeed, this assumption continues among many modern philosophers, all of whom reject the idea that Hobbes or Locke provides anything even remotely resembling an accurate account of original human societies. Many of them agree, however, that under ideal circumstances, agreement to a set of norms provides a justification for those norms. Thus, John Rawls has famously argued that if a set of political institutions would be agreed to by agents in an idealized "original position," then those institutions are just.

The idea that contracts are legitimate because they are agreed to by contracting parties is actually of relatively recent vintage. For example, it did not become the central organizing principle of the law of contracts until the late nineteenth century. Prior to that time, contract law was organized around the assumption that there were a number of consensual relationships—sale, hire, lease, bailment, etc.—each with its own set of rules that were socially imposed rather than individually authored by the agreement of the parties. Likewise, the principle that moral obligations are created by the agreement of the parties, which seemed self-evident to Hobbes and Locke, was deeply puzzling to earlier thinkers. The late scholastics gave the question the most thought. Agreement and promises seem to create moral obligations from nothing. I have no obligation to go to your dinner party, but if I agree to go to the dinner party, I have become morally culpable if I do not go. Such ex nihilio creation of moral requirements seemed the proper preserve of God—a suspect, Ockhamist God at that—rather than man. They concluded that the bare fact of agreement created no moral obligation. A criminal who breaks his promise to murder commits no wrong. Rather, agreement creates an obligation only if it aims at some laudatory end. It is the end and purposes of our agreements that create contractual obligations, not the bare fact of our choice. The difference between the social contract theorists and the late scholastics is more than merely semantic. For the earlier thinkers, we inhabit a moral universe that cannot be reduced to individuals and their choices. For the scholastic theorists, obligations arose as a matter of natural law, which in turn rested on the beneficent structure of the universe created by God. In short, we live in a normative world not of our own creation. It was already here when we arrived on the scene, and it is not contingent on our agreement for its authority.

Hobbes and Locke also use the language of natural law, but they mean something very different by it. Their ambition is to drill down to the normative foundations of society, which they conceptualize as ultimately individualistic. The foundations are individualistic because they rest on the agreement of individuals, at which point there is nothing more that can or need be said in their defense. On this view, we have become as the gods, not because we know good and evil, but because we create it.

Covenants

Adam and Eve do not exit the Garden through a social contract. Like the inhabitants of the state of nature, they have an anomalous moral status in the Garden, but it lies in the absence of sin, not in the absence of obligation. Indeed, they come into the Garden burdened with obligations. From the beginning, they are given care of the world and a duty to tend the Garden. They must be fruitful and multiply and replenish the earth. They must obey God's command not to eat of the forbidden tree of knowledge. How one reads the story of the Fall and assigns moral culpability to the characters in the narrative is a complex task with a complex history. Latter-day Saints have much to say on this; most notably, they offer a positive reading of Eve's choice. This drains the story of the misogyny often assigned to it by Christian theologies, but it means God's initial command not to partake is puzzling. Notice that in the Adam and Eve story in the Garden, none of their obligations arise as a result of their consent. Rather, obligations are imposed on them by God, and they never occupy a condition where these obligations are not present. The difference between the story of Eden and the story of social contract is ultimately conceptual rather than historical. As I noted above, social contract theorists don't believe that they are describing historical events. Likewise, the story of Adam and Eve is a highly stylized narrative that is as much about ritual and theology as anything that today we would recognize as history. As the success of Rawlsian philosophy demonstrates, state-of-nature stories, repackaged as the original position, retain their hold because they present a conceptual possibility, namely of a choosing agent bereft of obligation, save those freely chosen. For Genesis, such a vision of humanity is incoherent. To be human is to be a child of God and an inhabitant of his creation, subject to his commands and the demands of his creation. Authority arises not from within the self but from outside of it.

Upon their expulsion from Eden, Adam and Eve entered into covenants with God. Again, the presence of agreement tempts us toward reading obligations through the lens of social contract. The covenant of Adam and Eve with God, however, does not found their obligations to one another or to God. Such obligations already existed, and having left Eden, the problem faced by Adam and Eve is not generating obligations in some kind of a normative state of nature. Rather, Adam and Eve face the problem of sin and redemption. Through the Fall they have alienated themselves from God and offended against his laws. Being mortal and imperfect, they can expect to do so again. God's covenant offers them redemption. It is not a contract between equals that establishes a self-contained normative world defined by subjective choice. Rather, it is a gift. In the scriptures, the images used to describe God's covenant with his people revolve around families rather than contracts. We are adopted by covenant into the House of Israel. God's covenant with his people is likened to the marriage of a faithful bridegroom to a faithless bride. Through the covenant of the Atonement, believers become joint heirs with Christ. Adoption, marriage, heirship. These are all examples of what jurists call status rather than contract. They each carry a bundle of rights and obligations, but those rights and obligations are not authored by the parties to the covenant. They come attached to social roles that are inherited and whose content has been defined by past practice and tradition. As a gift and a status, rather than a self-authored contract, covenant sits more easily within a conservative than a liberal, or certainly a progressive, disposition. The logic of covenant trades on the presumed coherence and legitimacy of externally defined roles that make sense of our relationship to God. The imagery of covenant thus rejects the progressive disposition's stance toward both time and authority.

Conclusion

This is not an essay about politics, at least not directly. Latter-day Saints in the United States tend to identify with the Republican Party and might therefore be identified as politically center-right or right-wing. Most Latter-day Saints, however, do not reside in the United States, and non-American Latter-day Saints are as likely to identify with political parties of the left as of the right. Likewise, even within the United States, a minority of Latter-day Saints identify with the Democratic Party. Furthermore, in the topsy-turvy world of American political ideology, there is nothing particularly conservative in a dispositional sense about contemporary right-wing politics. Regardless, my goal in this essay is not to justify, criticize, or even explain the political allegiances of Latter-day Saints in theological terms. Political behavior has multiple causes, including demographics, economic conditions, geographical location, and even political personalities, none of which are directly related to religious beliefs. It seems an obvious mistake to think that political behavior is determined by theological arguments.

Furthermore, political parties are only indirectly vehicles of political thought. In a democracy, they ultimately exist to win elections and coordinate the actions of elected officials. They are vehicles for creating coalitions or advancing the goals of charismatic leaders. In doing this, they may be aided by ideology. Such party ideologies are a kind of political thought, even if a generally degenerate form. In successful political parties, however, ideology will be compromised in the process of coalition building. We often deride our politicians for a lack of principle, but the exigencies of democratic institutions force such compromises upon them. If we accept the legitimacy of such institutions, then a certain flexibility of principles among elected officials is a virtue rather than a vice. It does suggest, however, that creating theological apologia for the Democratic or Republican parties is a fool's errand. Party ideologies aren't produced by a process calculated to generate intellectual depth or coherence.

There is obviously *some* relationship between dispositions and political ideologies, but it would be a mistake to think that there is a straight line from basic prejudices to a political program. This is perhaps especially true in the current political moment in which political ideologies and coalitions that have remained relatively stable for decades are being reshuffled by populism on the right and by an at-times anti-liberal progressivism. Dispositions can also be blended when it comes to political ideologies. Conservative liberalism is a perfectly coherent possibility, as demonstrated by numerous liberal factions in center-right political parties around the world. Likewise, some political ideologies, such as "Red Toryism" in the UK and certain kinds of environmentalism, might best be described as progressive conservatism. One can also make a distinction between personal or political projects and political or legal institutions. In my opinion, societies perform best when conservative or progressive political projects are pursued within the context of liberal political and legal institutions.

Both conservatism and progressivism have turned pernicious when they are unshackled by such institutions. On the other hand, I believe that liberalism is a poor basis on which to structure personal relationships. This is especially true within families, where obligations often exceed any commitments that can be plausibly ascribed to consent or contract. Certainly, every disposition creates risks. A conservative disposition risks a certain insouciance toward injustice. Liberal prejudices tend toward a flattened vision of human beings and their relationships that often misses important sources of humanity and human meaning. A progressive disposition can tend toward a destructive disdain for traditions and communities that can appear in the progressive imagination as nothing more than sites of injustice. These possibilities and dangers are worth remembering in those moments when we reflect, as in this essay, on the prejudices that always structure our thought.

With all those caveats, the gospel as taught by the Latter-day Saints is not another option to be legitimized by the awesome normative force of our individual choice. Nor is it a project of perpetual liberation from the tyranny of our situatedness. Rather, it is a gift to be cherished in gratitude from a God to whom we always already owe obedience.

CHAPTER 7

Joseph Smith and Mormon Theologies of Religious Pluralism

The brute fact of religious pluralism is one of the central features of modern liberal democracies. Secular defenders of liberalism often implicitly assume that religious traditions lack the internal resources to interact respectfully and peacefully with other religious traditions.[1] The quintessential religious response to pluralism is taken to be violent crusade or jihad. To be sure, religious believers in liberal democracies often have respectful, friendly, and productive interactions across religious divides in practice, but this only works in secularist theory because such people are good liberals but bad believers.[2] This caricature of religious believers fails to acknowledge the often deep and complex engagement of religious traditions with the fact of religious pluralism and ignores the internal resources of those traditions for peaceful and generous interactions across religious divides. This essay examines some of those internal resources within the Latter-day Saint tradition by looking at ideas of religious pluralism in the thought of Mormonism's founding prophet, Joseph Smith. Neither Smith nor contemporary Latter-day Saints have ever produced a comprehensive

---

1. The philosopher Robert Audi provides a measured example of this concern:

> [V]ery commonly those who identify with what they regard as the ultimate Divine source of religious reasons believe that anyone who does not identify with it is forsaken, damned, or in some other way fundamentally deficient. This disapproval is often enhanced or even inflamed by others openly rejecting the relevant command or standard, as is common in, for example, sexual matters. Nor are religious people always consoled by knowledge that the disagreement with their religiously inspired views is respectful; this can be so even if they think those rejecting the views do so on the basis of their religious convictions following a false god or misunderstanding the true one can be even worse than secular error.

Robert Audi, *Religious Commitment and Secular Reason* (Cambridge University Press, 2000), 101.

2. For example, during Mitt Romney's run for the US Presidency, Damon Linker suggested that Americans had nothing to fear from Romney's faith only so long as he was a "lukewarm believer." Damon Linker, "The Big Test," *The New Republic*, January 15, 2007, https://newrepublic.com/article/63193/the-big-test.

theology of religious pluralism. However, an examination of the teachings of Mormonism's founder reveals a generous and largely positive stance toward religious pluralism, perhaps especially across the divide between Christians and non-Christians.

Smith organized The Church of Jesus Christ of Latter-day Saints in 1830, and he was accepted by his followers as a "prophet, seer, and revelator." He produced hundreds of pages of new scripture that Latter-day Saints accept, alongside the Christian bible, as canonical. Because Smith's ministry occurred in the early nineteenth century, Latter-day Saints and scholars of Mormonism are fortunate in having a wealth of documents from the foundational moment of the tradition. Smith, however, was not a systematic theologian. He never made any effort to provide a complete account of his religious vision. Rather, he left a heterogeneous collection of scriptural texts, letters, sermons, and occasional newspaper articles. Within this mass of materials, there are at least three places where themes of religious pluralism emerge: attitudes toward Judaism, the intrusion of the United States Constitution into Latter-day Saint scripture, and religious pluralism within Smith's theocratic imagination.

An Independent Jewish Eschatology

Joseph Smith's religious thought is not notable for its interest in abstract nouns. Rather, his theological imagination focused on narrative, ritual, ecclesiastical authority, and communal organization. One will search Smith's religious oeuvre in vain for explicit disquisitions on religious pluralism. Thinking on this question does appear, however, in what may strike modern readers as an unlikely place: eschatology. Mormonism was born into the religious world of the Second Great Awakening, where Christian interest in the end of the world and the millennial reign of justice associated with the promised Second Coming of Jesus Christ was intense. Most dramatically, the Baptist preacher William Miller predicted that the world would end with the Second Coming of Christ on October 22, 1844. His prediction proved inaccurate, but the so-called Millerites went on to form the Seventh-day Adventist movement. Like Miller, Smith was intensely interested in the eschaton, but in contrast to most of his contemporaries, he thought of the end of the world in terms of space rather than time. Hence, where Miller predicted the date of Christ's reappearing, Smith's religious imagination focused on where Christ was to appear and the nature of that place.

While eschatology superficially seems to be an esoteric mapping of future history, within Christianity the Second Coming of Christ provides a kind of theory of justice. The millennial kingdom at the end of time will realize a perfected world where the lamb will lie down with the lion and swords will be beaten into plowshares (Isa. 2:4; 11:16). Hence, to imagine the end of the world is to imagine what a perfectly just world would look like. This is particularly true of Joseph Smith, who turned away from questions of historical chronology to focus on building a just society, what he called Zion, in preparation for the Second Coming of Jesus Christ.

The earliest discussion of Zion in Latter-day Saint scripture comes in the Book of Mormon. Published in 1830, the Book of Mormon is the longest and most elaborate of Joseph Smith's scriptural productions. It is a sprawling narrative that purports to be the record of ancient prophets who are frequently looking forward to the last days in which Smith, his followers, and modern Latter-day Saints take themselves to be living. Within that narrative, an ancient prophet named Ether predicts that in the last days Zion, the city of God, will be built on the American continent by the gathering of the Gentiles (Ether 13:2–4). The effort to create this Zion preoccupied Smith for the rest of his ministry, as he taught Latter-day Saint converts to gather together and begin work on the construction of the city of God. This vision of Zion provided the axis around which Smith and his followers organized their movement. Hence, for example, Smith's later published revelations contain much more material on the nature of property holdings in the city of God than they do on matters of ordinary ecclesiastical concern, such as congregational structure or patterns of Sunday worship.[3] In this sense, Ether's prophecy oriented Smith's ministry toward the creation of a just society, conceptualized as Zion. Zion in turn was perched at the edge of the eschaton. On one hand, Zion was to be the literal germ of the Kingdom of God at the end of time. On the other hand, Zion was to be a concrete settlement located on the then American frontier, a social experiment in religious communitarianism of the kind common in Jacksonian America.[4]

3. See Nathan B. Oman, *Law and the Restoration: Law and Latter-Day Saint Thought and Scripture* (Greg Kofford Books, 2024), 163–80 (discussing Joseph Smith's revelation dealing with property ownership).

4. See generally Leonard J. Arrington, Feramorz Y. Fox, and Dean L. May, *Building the City of God: Community and Cooperation Among the Mormons*, 2nd ed. (University of Illinois Press, 1992).

Within the Book of Mormon, the place of Judaism within the eschatology of Zion becomes perhaps the earliest site of Latter-day Saint discourse about religious pluralism.[5] For the monotheisms of Islam and Christianity, Judaism occupies an important conceptual role. It is the religious other that cannot be imagined away precisely because Christians are committed in some sense to the authority of the Hebrew scriptures, and Jews appear in the Qur'an as fellow monotheists and characters from the Hebrew scripture inhabit the revelations of Muhammed. As Remi Brague has noted, "Later religions (or 'daughter religions') all face the same problem: they have to position themselves in relation to the mother religion—or mother religions, if there were several. This problem had its effect on sacred texts. Each text or group of texts refers back to a prehistory."[6] This dynamic is on full display in the Book of Mormon, whose narrative and theologies are positioned in relationship to both Jewish and Christian scripture. The narrative takes both the covenant of God with Israel and the Christian story of Jesus's resurrection and promised return at the end of time as central.

In the evangelical Christianity that defined the religious mainstream of Joseph Smith's America, the dominant theological approach to Judaism was supersessionist. With the advent of Christianity, God's covenant with Israel had been decisively replaced by the rise of the church, which became the sole receptacle of God's promises to Israel. In its darkest form, supersessionism cast Jews as primary villains in the Christian story, leading to such antisemitic tropes as the blood libel and the long history of Christian mistreatment of Jews. However, supersessionism could also take a more "benign" form, casting modern Jews as mere victims of an obsolete religion in need of Christian conversion. This benign supersessionism manifested itself in such projects as the American Society of Evangelizing the Jews and The American Society for Meliorating the Condition of the Jews, which counted James Monroe and John Quincy Adams as members of its governing board. Many of Smith's followers and his associates in the leadership of the infant Mormon movement adopted this benign form of supersessionism, advocating aggressive Mormon proselytizing of Jews.[7]

5. See Steven Epperson, *Mormons and Jews: Early Mormon Theologies of Israel* (Signature Books, 1992), 19–42 (discussing Judaism within the Book of Mormon).

6. Rémi Brague, *The Law of God: The Philosophical History of an Idea*, translated by Lydia G. Cochrane (University of Chicago Press, 2007), 85.

7. See Epperson, *Mormons and Jews*, 113–38 (discussing disagreements over supersessionism within the early Latter-day Saint movement).

The Book of Mormon, however, rejects supersessionism. Within its narrative of the last days, Christ's advent does not mark the end of God's covenant with Israel, nor have God's promises to Israel been transferred to a new Gentile church. Rather, the Book of Mormon repeatedly emphasizes God's continued faithfulness to His "ancient covenant people" and reaffirms the validity of Israel's covenant with God notwithstanding the advent of Jesus Christ.[8] Rather, the Book of Mormon explicitly rejects Christian antisemitism based on supersessionist theology. Speaking to modern Latter-day Saints, a Book of Mormon prophet says, "Yea, and ye need not any longer hiss, nor spurn, nor make game of the Jews, nor any of the remnant of the house of Israel; for behold, the Lord remembereth his covenant unto them, and he will do unto them according to that which he hath sworn" (3 Ne. 29:8). In the last days, Book of Mormon prophets state that God will do a "marvelous work and a wonder" among the Gentiles (2 Ne. 27:26). This was to be the foundation and rise of the Church. At the same time, God would continue faithful to Israel, working out their salvation independent of His latter-day work among the Gentiles. The Book of Mormon presents a kind of two-track eschatology, one for the Jews and one for the Gentiles. If we take eschatology to present a view of cosmic justice, the earliest Latter-day Saint eschatology thus inscribes religious pluralism based around Judaism into its vision of God's final design for the world.

This two-track eschatology had implications for Joseph Smith's attitudes toward Judaism. In January, 1836 Smith engaged Joshua Seixas to teach Hebrew in the "School of the Prophets," a Mormon lyceum established in Kirtland, Ohio.[9] Seixas was the son of American Jewish royalty. His father, Gershom Seixas, had participated in George Washington's inauguration and was a trustee of Columbia University. Smith was fascinated and impressed by Seixas, and the Latter-day Saint prophet's initial impulse was to attempt to convert him to Mormonism. After Seixas

8. Speaking to modern Gentiles, a Book of Mormon prophet writes:

> O ye Gentiles, have ye remembered the Jews, mine ancient covenant people? Nay; but ye have cursed them, and have hated them, and have not sought to recover them. But behold, I will return all these things upon your own heads; for I the Lord have not forgotten my people (2 Ne. 29:5).

9. See generally Louis C. Zucker, "Joseph Smith as a Student of Hebrew," *Dialogue: A Journal of Mormon Thought* 3, no. 2 (1968): 41–55; Moshe Davis, "The Holy Land Idea in American Spiritual History," in *With Eyes Toward Zion: Scholars Colloquium on America-Holy Land Studies*, edited by Moshe Davis (Arno Press, 1977), 3–33.

tactfully deflected his awkward efforts at evangelism, Smith abandoned them. More strikingly, he seems to have largely abandoned the idea of evangelizing Jews, rejecting proposals by his associates to call Mormon missionaries tasked with converting Jews to Mormonism.[10] Rather than missionary work on the model of the American Society for Meliorating the Condition of the Jews, he ultimately sent Orson Hyde, a member of the Church's Quorum of the Twelve Apostles and thus a top Latter-day Saint leader, on a mission to Jerusalem. After an arduous journey from Nauvoo, Illinois, to the Holy Land, Hyde ascended the Mount of Olives and offered a prayer dedicating the land to the return of the Jews.[11]

There are two things worth noting about Hyde's mission to Palestine. First, in comparison to evangelical efforts to convert Jews, it is remarkably passive. This is what Joseph Smith endorsed in place of a Latter-day Saint version of the American Society of Evangelizing the Jews. Second, it is tempting to read the meaning of Hyde's mission in terms of modern Zionism. Certainly, Hyde and Smith were vaguely aware of the proto-Zionism percolating in some Jewish circles. But Hyde's trip to Jerusalem came in 1841, more than a half century before Theodore Herzl's publication of *The Jewish State* launched modern Zionism. Since the foundation of the State of Israel in 1948, the Church has insisted that Hyde's ritual does not constitute an endorsement of Zionism.[12] Rather, Hyde's quixotic

---

10. See Epperson, *Mormons and Jews*, 88–89.

11. Epperson, 139–72; Davis, "The Holy Land Idea in American Spiritual History," 21–22.

12. In the 1970s, the Church created a small park on the Mount of Olives in Jerusalem where Hyde gave his dedicatory prayer. In explaining Hyde's act, then-apostle Howard W. Hunter, who later became president of the Church, said:

> We have members of the Church in the Muslim world. . . . Sometimes they are offended by members of the Church who give the impression that we favor only the aims of the Jews. The Church has an interest in all of Abraham's descendants, and we should remember that the history of the Arabs goes back to Abraham through his son Ishmael. . . . At the present time we are engaged in a project of beautifying the Mount of Olives in Jerusalem by a garden, in memory of Orson Hyde, an early apostle of the Church, and the dedicatory prayer he offered on that site. It is not because we favor one people over another. Jerusalem is sacred to the Jews, but it is also sacred to the Arabs. . . . Both the Jews and the Arabs are children of our Father. They are both children of promise, and as a church we do not take sides.

Howard W. Hunter, "All Are Alike unto God," *Ensign*, June 1979.

journey to Palestine should be seen as a ritualization of the independent Jewish eschatology of the Book of Mormon. It was, in effect, the concretizing of a theology of religious pluralism by men—Smith and Hyde—far more comfortable with ritual than abstract theorizing as an expression of a religious world view.

The Intrusion of the US Constitution into Latter-day Saint Scripture

The intrusion of the US Constitution into Latter-day Saint scripture marks another place where religious pluralism appears in the thought of Joseph Smith. The partial sacralization of the constitution in Latter-day Saint scripture came in response to violent persecution of the Latter-day Saints and how that experience altered their relationship with non-Mormon neighbors. Shortly after he organized the Church, Smith announced a revelation locating Zion in Jackson County, Missouri, near present-day Kansas City (see D&C 57:14). Latter-day Saint converts gathered to Missouri where they tried to implement a communitarian economic regime and await the expected return of Jesus Christ. This Latter-day Saint community drew forth the ire of non-Morman neighbors. Persecution began with directed violence against individuals that grew into widespread mob violence that ultimately drove the Latter-day Saints from Jackson County in 1833.[13]

The Saints relocated to a remote corner of northwestern Missouri, where events repeated themselves.[14] Mobs again attacked the Latter-day Saints, Mormon women were raped, and after a pitched battle between a Latter-day Saint militia and their attackers in 1838, the Missouri governor issued an executive order declaring "the Mormons must be treated as enemies, and must be exterminated or driven from the State if necessary for the public peace."[15] Three days later, the Missouri militia massacred all of the inhabitants of the Latter-day Saint hamlet of Haun's Mill. Joseph Smith and other church leaders were arrested on a charge of treason and in effect held as hostages to ensure that the Latter-day Saints vacated the state, which they did in the dead of winter, arriving as refugees in Illinois. Subsequently, Smith and his associates were allowed to escape after it

---

13. See Richard Lyman Bushman, *Joseph Smith: Rough Stone Rolling* (Alfred A. Knopf, 2005), 222–27.

14. See generally Stephen C. LeSueur, *The 1838 Mormon War in Missouri* (University of Missouri Press, 1987).

15. Quoted in Bushman, *Rough Stone Rolling*, 365.

became clear that the Saints had been driven from the state and the leaders of the mob would be able to expropriate their property.

In 1833, the Jackson County mob attracted widespread revulsion. People with little sympathy for the Saints' theology were nevertheless horrified at the spectacle of a religious minority persecuted for their faith and dispossessed of their property, and responded positively to Latter-day Saint appeals for sympathy. As one historian has written:

> The success of the appeal changed the Saints' relation to the world. The customary language of conversion and gathering implicitly conceived of non-Mormons as potential converts who accepted or rejected the missionaries' message. When a town rejected them, missionaries washed the dust off their feet and left that people to their fate. The persecution story, by contrast, recognized an unbaptized, sympathetic middle group, not joiners or enemies, but somewhere in between. Accounts of persecution, paradoxically, bridged the gulf between the Saints and the unbelieving world by envisioning a body of sympathetic others with whom friendly relations could be established without converting them.[16]

This idea of friendship appears within Smith's revelations through the sanctification of a shared commitment to the religious freedom protected by the constitution. In the pre–Civil War era its provisions provided no legal protection against local governments, but they did provide a shared political language that the Latter-day Saints could employ with their neighbors.

Within Smith's revelations, there is a shift from the apocalyptic time of the pre-1833 revelations to the historically situated time of the post-1833 revelations. Prior to 1833, the revelations imagine America as a political blank space in which to work out God's latter-day purposes. Within the text of the revelations, the United States and its institutions are invisible. On August 6, 1833, however, they enter Latter-day Saint scripture when Smith recorded a revelation stating, "[T]hat law of the land which is constitutional, supporting that principle of freedom in maintaining rights and privileges, belongs to all mankind, and is justifiable before me" (D&C 98:5). A few months later, Smith dictated a second revelation endorsing the US Constitution. In that text, God proclaims:

> According to the laws and constitution of the people which I have suffered to be established, and should be maintained, for the rights and protection of all flesh, according to just and holy principles. . . . And for this purpose have

16. Bushman, 227.

I established the Constitution of this land by the hands of wise men, whom I raised up unto this very purpose . . . (D&C 101:77–80).

With these passages, the US Constitution made its way into Latter-day Saint scripture. Both revelations were contained in the first edition of the Doctrine and Covenants in 1835, and they have remained part of the Latter-day Saint canon since that time.

There are a number of things worth noting about these passages. First, they do not provide a blanket endorsement of the United States or its constitution. If anything, the texts of Smith's revelations implicitly assume that the legitimacy of human law is doubtful.[17] After explaining "that principle of freedom" within the constitution is "justifiable before me," the voice of God in Smith's text continues, "Therefore, I, the Lord, justify you, and your brethren of my church, in befriending that law which is the constitutional law of the land," (D&C 98:6) suggesting some doubt as to the propriety of befriending human laws. Smith's revelations are thus not a bit of boilerplate religious patriotism. They are a cautious engagement with American law that picks out a single principle of religious freedom. Second, the principle of religious freedom identified within the revelation is not presented as a special providential act in favor of Smith and his followers. Rather, it "belongs to all mankind" (D&C 98:5). Finally, the texts had concrete implications for Latter-day Saint practice.

Once established in Nauvoo, Illinois, the Latter-day Saints, at Smith's instigation, inscribed their commitment to religious freedom in local law, passing a municipal ordinance declaring, "That the Catholics, Presbyterians, Methodists, Baptists, Latter-Day-Saints, Quakers, Episcopalieans [*sic*] Universalits [*sic*] Unitarians, Mahommedans, and all other religious sects and denominations whatever, shall have free toleration and equal Privilieges [*sic*] in this city."[18] The law went on to protect religious believers not only from government action but also private hostility motivated by religious animus. "[S]hould any person be guilty of ridiculing abusing, or otherwise depreciating another in consequence of

17. See generally Nathan B. Oman, "'I Will Give Unto You My Law': Section 42 as a Legal Text and the Paradoxes of Divine Law," in *Embracing the Law: Reading Doctrine and Covenants 42*, edited by Jeremiah John and Joseph M. Spencer (Neal A. Maxwell Institute for Religious Scholarship, 2017).

18. An Ordinance in relation to religious Societies, March 1, 1841, reproduced in Nauvoo City Council Minute Book, 1841–1845, p. 13, The Joseph Smith Papers, https://www.josephsmithpapers.org/paper-summary/nauvoo-city-council-minute-book-1841-1845/19.

his religion . . . shall on conviction thereof . . . be considered a disturber of the public peace, and fined . . . or imprisoned."[19] In dispensing with a "state action requirement," the ordinance went beyond the scope of the First Amendment, condemning private religious hostility. In other words, religious toleration was taken to be a personal imperative, not simply a limitation on the government's ability to target religion.

Religious Pluralism in Joseph Smith's Theocratic Imagination

In the nineteenth century, the Latter-day Saint idea of Zion always involved the gathering of the Saints to form a religious commonwealth. There was thus always a theocratic aspect of Smith's Zion theology, and fear of Mormon theocracy was one of the drivers of anti-Mormon violence. That violence, in turn, radicalized the Latter-day Saints, convincing them that their only hope for safety and peace was an independent, Latter-day Saint commonwealth beyond the reach of hostile outsiders. Violence against the Saints was also taken as evidence of the crescendoing wickedness of "the World," particularly the United States. This rising wickedness, in turn, was taken as evidence of the imminent return of Jesus Christ, although until the very end of his life Smith resolutely refused to give a specific timeline for the end of the world. Nevertheless, Mormon Zion-building and political maneuvering merged conceptually into Latter-day Saint eschatology, even though the concern of Smith and his associates tended to focus on immediate practical challenges.

As early as 1833, the Saints had turned to the idea of political independence as a solution to the problem of religious persecution. After their expulsion from Jackson County, Missouri, near present-day Kansas City, Smith and his followers relocated to the remote northwest corner of the state where a "Mormon county" was created for them, granting a very limited local autonomy within the state of Missouri for a time.[20] When mob violence again engulfed the Latter-day Saints, they relocated to Illinois, where the state legislature granted a charter to the City of Nauvoo that gave the Saints independence from local government.[21] As events in

---

19. An Ordinance in relation to religious Societies, March 1, 1841.

20. See Bushman, *Rough Stone Rolling*, 343–46.

21. See James L. Kimball Jr., "Protecting Nauvoo by Illinois Charter in 1840," in *Sustaining the Law: Joseph Smith's Legal Encounters*, edited by Gordon A. Madsen, Jeffrey N. Walker, and John W. Welch (BYU Studies, 2014), 297–308.

Nauvoo spiraled out of control, however, Smith instituted an even more radical framework for Latter-day Saint political autonomy.

In March, 1844, Smith organized "The Kingdom of God and his Laws, with the keys and powers thereof and judgment in the hands of his servants Ahman Christ," which came to be referred to as the Council of Fifty.[22] The Council was a group of ecclesiastical and civic leaders who discussed and planned Latter-day Saint political strategy. Their immediate goal was to resettle the Latter-day Saints someplace in the interior of North America beyond the reach of state and federal governments. Once there, their goal was to establish The Kingdom of God, a theocratic polity that would be transformed with the Second Coming of Christ into God's millennial kingdom at the end of time. Most of their deliberations focused on questions such as the pros and cons of various sites for settlement, relations with Native Americans, the maneuverings of state and federal authorities, and other such immediate concerns. Amid these practicalities, however, Smith and his followers were also trying to imagine the concrete shape of an ideal godly community.[23]

Partly from practical considerations and partly from theological imperative, Smith included three non-Mormons in the Council of Fifty. On April 11, 1844, he explained the reason for their membership. The

---

22. The minutes of the Council of Fifty during the lifetime of Joseph Smith and in the period immediately after his death have recently been published. See Matthew J. Grow et al., eds., *Administrative Records: Council of Fifty Minutes, March 1844–January 1846*, The Joseph Smith Papers (Church Historian's Press, 2016). The Council of Fifty as organized by Joseph Smith ceased to function after the Saints relocated to the Great Basin. A second Council of Fifty was organized by Church leaders in the 1880s, during the anti-polygamy crusades as a forum for political discussion among top Church leaders and as a way of coordinating the Latter-day Saint political response to the federal legal campaign. By the time the Church issued the so-called Manifesto in 1890 publicly abandoning the practice of plural marriage, this second Council of Fifty had ceased to function. Documents on this second Council of Fifty are collected in Jedediah Smart Rogers and Klaus J. Hansen, eds., *The Council of Fifty: A Documentary History* (Signature Books, 2014).

23. For general discussion of the Council of Fifty, see Matthew J. Grow and R. Eric Smith, eds., *The Council of Fifty: What the Records Reveal about Mormon History* (Religious Studies Center, Brigham Young University & Deseret Book, 2017); Klaus J. Hansen, *Quest for Empire: The Political Kingdom of God and the Council of Fifty in Mormon History* (University of Nebraska Press, 1974); D. Michael Quinn, "The Council of Fifty and Its Members, 1844 to 1945," *Brigham Young University Studies* 20, no. 3 (1980): 163–97.

inclusion of members "who are not members of the church of Jesus Christ of Latter Day Saints [and] neither profess any creed or religious sentiment whatever" was to emphasize "that we act on the broad and liberal principal [*sic*] that all men have equal rights, and ought to be respected, and that every man has a privilege in this organization of choosing for himself voluntarily his God, and what he pleases for his religion."[24] He went on to offer three reasons for the religiously pluralistic theocracy dreamed of by the Latter-day Saints in the Council of Fifty.

First, he argued that the approach to God requires religious pluralism. "God cannot save or damn a man only on the principle that every man acts, chooses and worships for himself," he taught in April 1844.[25] This argument paralleled the justification given in an 1833 revelation endorsing the US Constitution's protection of religious freedom. Those protections existed, said the revelation, "that every many may act in doctrine and principle pertaining to futurity, according to the moral agency which I have given unto him, that every many may be accountable for his own sins in the day of judgment" (D&C 101:78). Within a context of pluralism and choice, Smith taught that "there is no danger but that every man will embrace the light."[26] Hence, rather than seeing religious pluralism as a threat to religious purity, Smith saw such pluralism as its precondition. Religious choice required alternatives, and without religious choice true faithfulness to God was not possible.

Second, Smith saw religious hostility as a virulent force in human history. The spirit of "bigotry and intollerance [*sic*] towards a mans religious sentiments . . . has drenched the earth with blood."[27] By 1844, when Smith spoke these words to the Council of Fifty, he had extensive firsthand experience with religious violence. He had been tarred and feathered in Ohio, his followers had been murdered and dispossessed in Missouri, and he had been driven into hiding in Illinois to escape those bent on his destruction. The plans of the Council of Fifty to escape to the west might be seen as a retreat from religious pluralism, an effort to create peace by avoiding religious difference through sheer distance.[28] In the context of those plans, it is

24. Grow et al., *Administrative Records: Council of Fifty Minutes, March 1844–January 1846*, 97.

25. Grow et al., 97.

26. Grow et al., 97.

27. Grow et al., 97–101.

28. The argument that early Mormon history should be read in terms of a retreat from religious pluralism has been made most forcefully in Marvin S. Hill, *Quest*

striking that Smith saw the solution in terms of cultivating a more generous attitude toward religious pluralism rather than its elimination.

Finally, Smith linked religious pluralism with the cultivation of the soul. He saw religious bigotry and intolerance as a temptation to sin. "When a man feels the least temptation to such intolerance he ought to spurn it from him."[29] Five years earlier, Smith had spent a miserable winter in the damp, unheated basement of a jail in Liberty, Missouri. From that prison cell, he had written a letter to his followers that expanded on this theme. Having denounced those who drove the Saints from Missouri, he turned the attention of his followers to their own capacity for religious bigotry. "[W]e ought always to be aware of those prejudices which sometimes so strangly [*sic*] presented themselves and are so congenial to human nature against our nieghbors [*sic*] friends and brethren of the world who choose to differ with us in opinion and in matters of faith."[30] For Smith, however, being on the guard against the natural human tendency toward religious tribalism and hostility was not simply a prophylaxis against religious conflict. Rather, it was part of the process of purifying the soul in the imitation of God. Delicately threading the needle between the demands of religious solidarity and a generous pluralism, he wrote:

> There is a ty [*sic*] from God that should be exercised towards those of our faith who walk uprightly which is peculiar to itself but it is without prejudice but gives scope to the mind which inables us to conduct ourselves with grater liberality to-wards all others that are not of our faith than what they exercise towards one another these principals approximate nearer to the mind of God because it is like God or God like.[31]

By insisting on non-Mormon members within "The Kingdom of God and his Laws, with the keys and powers thereof and judgment in the hands of his servants Ahman Christ," Smith inscribed the idea of generous religious pluralism into the Latter-day Saint vision of the City of God.

Anti-Mormons murdered Smith a few weeks after he delivered his address on religious pluralism to the Council of Fifty. After his death, the hardheaded Brigham Young took control of the Council of Fifty,

---

for Refuge: The Mormon Flight from American Pluralism (Signature Books, 1989).

29. Grow et al., *Administrative Records: Council of Fifty Minutes, March 1844–January 1846*, 101.

30. Letter to Edward Partridge and the Church, circa 22 March 1839, p. 8, The Joseph Smith Papers, https://www.josephsmithpapers.org/paper-summary/letter-to-edward-partridge-and-the-church-circa-22-march-1839/8.

31. Letter to Edward Partridge and the Church, circa 22 March 1839, p. 8.

the non-Mormon members were dropped or turned against the Saints, and the organization became focused on the practical organization of the Latter-day Saint exodus to the Great Basin before being dissolved by Young. During Mormonism's existential crisis of the mid-1840s, Young created a more hierarchical, authoritarian, and administratively effective Latter-day Saint community. However, he continued his theological allegiance to Smith's vision of a pluralistic, millennial theocracy. In an 1867 sermon, he taught:

> Some suppose that when the Kingdom of God governs on the earth, everybody who does not belong to the Church of Jesus Christ will be persecuted and killed. This is as false an idea as can exist. . . . [I]t is not so in the Kingdom of God; it is not so with the law nor with the Priesthood of the Son of God. You can believe in one God, or in three gods, or in a thousand gods; you can worship the sun or the moon, or a stick or a stone, or anything you please. Are not all mankind the workmanship of the hands of God? And does he not control the workmanship of His hands? They have the privilege of worshipping as they please.[32]

Even as Young was delivering that sermon, however, Mormon theocracy as a political project was failing. The Saints never escaped the authority of the federal government, and in the decades after the Civil War, the power of that government would be deployed to force the Latter-day Saint commonwealth to conform to the political and social norms of the United States. Jesus Christ failed to return to the nineteenth-century Zion so arduously prepared for him by the Latter-day Saints, and the City of God and the literal Kingdom of God were pushed into an ever-delayed eschaton. Despite this failure, Smith's vision of religious pluralism continued to echo within the Latter-day Saints' vision of an ideal community. That ideal community, however, was transformed from a concrete political project into a more flexible moral ideal and an eschatological hope delayed to an ever-retreating end times.

Conclusion

Joseph Smith is that rare figure in human history, the successful founder of a new religious tradition. The America of the Second Great Awakening was planted thick with prophets and charismatic leaders. Smith, however, stands out for having created a church and a community of believers that

32. Brigham Young, *Journal of Discourses* (Latter-day Saints' Book Depot, 1856), 12:113–14.

has endured and grown, claiming over seventeen million formal members today.[33] He was not, however, a systematic religious thinker. He continues to be a towering intellectual and spiritual presence in the movement that he founded, but it is perilous to draw a straight line from his teachings to current Latter-day Saint beliefs. Like any religious tradition, Mormonism is continually reinterpreting itself, including its founding stories and the teachings of its founding prophets. Hence, the ideas presented in this essay are less a survey of current Latter-day Saint beliefs than a sampling of some of the intellectual resources of their tradition.

Smith's positive stance toward religious pluralism and generous attitude toward the religious beliefs of others does find a place within current Latter-day Saint discourse. The most explicit modern theological pronouncement on religious pluralism came from the Church's governing First Presidency in a formal 1978 statement, which read:

> The great religious leaders of the world such as Mohammed, Confucius, and the Reformers, as well as philosophers including Socrates, Plato, and others, received a portion of God's light. Moral truths were given to them by God to enlighten whole nations and to bring a higher level of understanding to individuals.[34]

Within this theology, God is at work throughout the human race. The Church of Jesus Christ of Latter-day Saints, despite its strong claims to religious authority, is not the only conduit of God's revelation. Accordingly, Latter-day Saints can see religious pluralism as another mechanism by which to seek—in the language of Latter-day Saint scripture and ritual—"further light and knowledge."

---

33. "Statistics and Church Facts | Total Church Membership," Church Newsroom, accessed October 14, 2024, http://newsroom.churchofjesuschrist.org/facts-and-statistics. For theological reasons, the Church counts every person who has ever received Latter-day Saint baptism as "a member of the Church." Very large numbers of those people, however, are no longer observant members of the Church and many of them would no longer consider themselves Latter-day Saints. It is impossible to obtain accurate global information on the number of self-identified Latter-day Saints. It seems unlikely that it is more than half or at most two-thirds of the number of formal Church members, but this is purely speculative.

34. Quoted in Robert L. Millet, "The Eternal Gospel," *Ensign*, July 1996, https://www.lds.org/ensign/1996/07/the-eternal-gospel.

CHAPTER 8

The Perils of Constitutional Theology

Each year the United States Supreme Court produces a new batch of cases construing the religion clauses of the First Amendment. There is something stylized about the debates these cases inevitably provoke, as partisans on either side of the various fault lines of church-state thinking adapt the well-worn arguments of separationism, accommodation, religious freedom, and equality before the law to new situations. Almost all of these debates treat religion and the law as separate things, with the constitution deciding how far one will be allowed to dictate to the other.

What is often lost in these debates is the way in which religions use the constitution to define themselves. Law is not something that just happens to religion. Rather, religions use secular law to create theologies that both explain the faith to believers and justify the religion to often-suspicious outsiders. The United States began its life as an overwhelmingly Protestant country, one that was often hostile to non-Protestants. One of the most potent ways in which religious outsiders have defended their place in American society is by staking a religious claim to the US Constitution. In a sense, outsider religions have become American by developing theologies of the constitution.

Consider the Supreme Court's decision in *Espinoza v. Montana*, which declared so-called Blaine amendments unconstitutional. To understand the religious stakes in the case, one must consider the Catholic experience in America. Early in the nineteenth century, the Vatican, largely in response to French anti-clericalism, expressed hostility toward both liberalism and democracy. At the time, there were relatively few Catholics in the United States, but these statements inflamed the already deep-seated anti-Catholicism of American Protestants, crystallizing for many a vision of Catholics as implacably hostile to American democracy.

As the century progressed, Catholic immigration to the United States increased, first from Ireland and French Canada and later from southern and central Europe. In addition, America absorbed large Catholic populations in California and the southwest when it annexed those territories from Mexico. Despite the moderation of Rome's stance toward liberal democracy over the course of the nineteenth century, however, anti-Catholicism if anything increased with the growth of the Catholic population.

These fears galvanized Protestant America into emphasizing public schools as a vehicle to "Americanize" immigrants, a process that included a healthy dose of indoctrination in non-denominational Protestantism. Catholics created their own parochial school system in response, and in reaction states adopted so-called Blaine amendments, which prohibited any support for parochial schools. At the same time, mainly Protestant activists began pushing the idea that the constitution, which doesn't contain the term, embodied the ideal of the separation of church and state. Historically, the emphasis on separationism (as opposed to disestablishment) was new, and its partisans were clear in directing their ire primarily at Catholics.

My point in recounting this history is not to poison the well against separationism, which can be defended in good faith without anti-Catholicism. Rather, the history is necessary to see the way in which Catholic belonging in American society is tied up, in part, with the history of debates over the Blaine amendments. The response to the hostility represented by the Blaine amendments is telling. Long before Catholic lawyers and legal scholars began crafting doctrinal legal attacks on the amendments, Catholic thinkers such as John Courtney Murray, SJ (1904–1967) crafted theologies that accommodated religious freedom and pluralism. Building on the more moderate stance taken by the Papacy in the late nineteenth century, he made peace with the US Constitution.

This theological embrace of the constitution did three things. First, it helped lay to rest some of the hostility and suspicion directed at American Catholics. Second, it allowed at least some Catholics to offer a constitutional critique of America's de facto Protestant establishment. They were hardly the only or even the most important voices in this critique, but their embrace of a certain vision of the constitution contributed to the transformation of constitutional law. Finally, the theological embrace of the constitution transformed Catholicism itself, with the writings of Murray and other American theologians contributing to the revolution of Vatican II.

The theological embrace of the constitution is not without religious risks. Consider the case of the Latter-day Saints. While Mormonism began in upstate New York in the 1830s, the acceptance of The Church of Jesus Christ of Latter-day Saints by American society was a long time coming. During the 1830s and 1840s, Latter-day Saints were beaten, raped, and murdered by mobs convinced that Mormonism, like Catholicism, represented an existential threat to American democracy. The Latter-day

Saint embrace of polygamy in the 1840s and 1850s, physical and social isolation in the Great Basin, and the mass immigration of converts from abroad further inflamed hostility toward this "foreign" group. That hostility spawned a grueling series of legal and political battles that began in the late 1850s and didn't end until the LDS Church finally abandoned plural marriage between 1890 and 1904.

Unsurprisingly, the fortunes of the US Constitution within Mormon theology waxed and waned over the course of the nineteenth century. Early Latter-day Saint scriptures produced in response to the first round of anti-Mormon violence in the early 1830s embraced the idea of religious freedom in the constitution as a product of divine inspiration. As anti-Mormon violence peaked in the 1840s, however, Latter-day Saints soured on the American experiment. They embraced the ideal of political independence for a Latter-day Saint commonwealth in the far west and tried to emigrate to what was then a remote Mexican territory. The American conquest and annexation of northern Mexico in 1848, however, foiled these plans.

During the 1840s and the 1850s, Latter-day Saints were more likely to express bitter regret over the constitution's inability to protect religious minorities than to laud it as divinely inspired. As anti-Mormon lawyers replaced anti-Mormon mobs in the 1860s, 1870s, and 1880s, however, the Latter-day Saints rediscovered the usefulness of law and, with it, a reverence for the constitution. During the legal battles over polygamy, professionally trained Latter-day Saint lawyers fought a series of largely unsuccessful cases to the US Supreme Court. Their efforts nevertheless forestalled the final Latter-day Saint capitulation for two generations, pushing constitutional law into the foreground of Latter-day Saint experience and consciousness.

In the twentieth century the Latter-day Saints had to forge a new identity that could put the role of sullen and defeated "fanatics" firmly in the past. Among other strategies, they claimed their place as "regular" Americans by firmly embracing the idea of the constitution as divinely inspired. By inscribing Americanism deeply into their theological discourse, Latter-day Saints assured themselves that despite over a half-century of at-times violent conflict with the United States, it was religiously acceptable to be a "regular" American. At the same time, their religious enthusiasm for the constitution helped to reassure a skeptical nation that Latter-day Saints could be trusted as American citizens.

This theological enthusiasm for the constitution has been a mixed blessing for Mormonism. Many twentieth century Latter-day Saints tended to ignore the at best ambivalent embrace of the constitution in their nineteenth-century scriptures, instead elevating the constitution itself into a quasi-religious text. This was done despite the document's manifest moral failures, particularly in regard to slavery. A hyper veneration for the constitution contributed to a strain of ultra-right-wing politics within mid-twentieth-century Mormonism and may have delayed the formal excision of racism from Latter-day Saint practice and theology in 1978.

There have always been more moderate voices in Mormonism, such as US Solicitor General Rex Lee, who tempered the rush to canonize the constitution. As an institution, the contemporary LDS Church has generally seen reactionary mid-twentieth-century theologies as a liability to be discreetly abandoned. Nevertheless, the constitution as a sacred document continues to be a potent concept in American Latter-day Saint culture, and, like all scripture, the constitution can take on a religious life that wanders far from its text.

This can be seen in Utah's reaction to the COVID-19 pandemic. In some ways Utah was well served by Latter-day Saint culture, which places a high value on healthy lifestyles, young families, and functional institutions, all of which contributed to a society that ought to have been fairly resilient in the face of the pandemic. This can be seen in Utah's high rates of early COVID-19 testing and its relatively low death rate from infection.

However, over the summer of 2020 the rate of infection in Utah spiked dramatically. Large segments of Utah's population resisted calls for social distancing and the wearing of masks. Some ultra-conservatives in Utah vociferously insisted that such restrictions threatened the freedoms enshrined in the sacred scripture of the constitution. (These voices have been less clear about articulating precisely how public health rules violate constitutional law.) The political potency of this crude, religiously infused libertarianism almost certainly accounted for the anemic efforts of state officials in Utah to enforce social distancing. While the LDS Church itself was fairly aggressive about shutting down its own religious services, at least one member of the Church hierarchy likely threw fuel on the flames by suggesting that public health restrictions could threaten religious liberty.

This dynamic created a bizarre religious impasse in July 2020 when the regional leadership of the LDS Church in Utah issued a letter calling on all church members in the state to wear masks in public. Despite the stereotype of disciplined Latter-day Saints falling into line behind church leaders, the letter was met with fierce criticism by some conservative church members. They insisted that their religious duty to the sacred principles of the constitution trumped the claims of religious counsel from church leaders. In one of the most hierarchical religions in America, the theological authority of the constitution, it would seem, can outweigh the theological authority of the ecclesiastical hierarchy. It's an impasse that threatened both public health and the cohesion of the Latter-day Saint community, an unintended legacy of theologizing the constitution in order to claim belonging in American society.

The constitution is a legal document, but it is more than just a legal document. Throughout its history it has led a rich religious life. In many ways the story of the United States is the story of outsiders thrusting their way into society and claiming their place in the American mainstream. One of the ways religious outsiders have repeatedly done this is by claiming the constitution and working it into their theologies. Sometimes these internal interpretations of the constitution spill outward into the broader stream of constitutional law, as in *Espinoza v. Montana*. Always, the sacralization of the constitution helps to mediate membership in the American community. And sometimes constitutional theology has a darker side, turning into a destructive idol.

CHAPTER 9

Truth, Doctrine, and Authority

Mormonism is a very young religion. Approaching our bicentennial, we Latter-day Saints are religious and intellectual infants compared to other traditions. This is not without its virtues. There is an energy and dynamism to youth, as well as a sense of audacity and possibility. It does mean, however, that there is much in Mormon thought that is embryonic and yet to be worked out. The result for Latter-day Saint thinkers can be both excitement about the work yet to be done and confusion about apparently fundamental questions. Recently, a number of Latter-day Saint thinkers have turned their attention to the question of what constitutes church doctrine. Latter-day Saints are accustomed to speaking of their doctrine as though its contours and meaning are self-evident. Upon examination, however, this apparent simplicity proves deceptive. Indeed, the Church acknowledged this when it issued a widely discussed statement on "Approaching Mormon Doctrine," which noted the misunderstanding that resulted from a failure to consider the scope of the Church's doctrines without an appreciation of "the broad and complex context within which its doctrines have been declared."[1]

One example should suffice to illustrate the sorts of problems that arise when discussing the scope and claims of church doctrine. In the 1880s, Bishop Bunker of Bunkerville, Nevada, was excommunicated for apostasy. His apostasy consisted of publicly teaching against the doctrine that Adam was the father of Jesus Christ and the "only God with whom we have to do." This teaching, of course, was the famous Adam-God doctrine taught by Brigham Young. Less than thirty years later, however, the First Presidency under President Joseph F. Smith, along with the entire Quorum of the Twelve Apostles issued "The Father and the Son: A Doctrinal Exposition," more or less explicitly repudiating the Adam-God doctrine. Over the course of the twentieth century the teaching was repeatedly condemned by church leaders, making its way, for example, into Elder Bruce R. McConkie's list of "Seven Deadly Heresies."[2] This shift in teachings provokes a series of questions. Was the Adam-God doctrine ever

1. The Church of Jesus Christ of Latter-day Saints, "Approaching Mormon Doctrine," 2007, http://www.lds.org/ldsnewsroom/eng/commentary/approaching-mormon-doctrine.

2. See Bruce R. McConkie, "The Seven Deadly Heresies," *BYU Speeches* (blog), June 1, 1980, https://speeches.byu.edu/talks/bruce-r-mcconkie/seven-deadly-heresies/.

"official" church doctrine? Is it church doctrine now? How do we go about answering these questions? If church doctrine has shifted, does that mean that previous "official" doctrines were false? If church doctrine has proved mistaken in the past, how can we be certain of its reliability today?

Both Robert Millet and I have published essays that seek to grapple with some of these questions.[3] Both of us have focused our attention on the threshold question of how one determines whether any particular claim or teaching is church doctrine. If I understand him correctly, Millet believes that it is possible to offer a set of criteria that constitute necessary and sufficient conditions for any particular teachings to enjoy the status of church doctrine. The list of criteria that he offers—consistency across time, centrality, etc.—may defy a simple, mechanical application, but Millet seems to believe that it is possible in theory to identify conditions, what legal philosophers have called a "rule of recognition," that would define church doctrine. As a practical matter, the various markers of authenticity identified by Millet strike me as eminently sensible rules of thumb for discovering church doctrine. As a conceptual matter, however, I reject the idea that there is a rule of recognition for church doctrine. Put another way, I think that Millet's approach is pastorally useful but philosophically unsatisfying. I don't think that the authoritative can be sorted from the un-authoritative by applying a set of unchanging criteria. Rather, I think that authoritative church doctrine always emerges from the process of interpreting the totality of Latter-day Saint teachings and practices. We do not start from first principles but are necessarily always in the midst of an ongoing practice. In trying to figure out which parts of Mormonism have a heightened claim upon us—what is "doctrine" and what is mere "culture" or "opinion"—I think that we begin with those claims that no well-socialized Latter-day Saint can plausibly deny are church doctrine. Such claims exist, I believe, as a kind of brute fact, much in the way that a language presents certain brute facts to well-informed speakers of the language. Whatever one's theories of botany, biology, and zoology, any well-informed English speaker knows that it does violence to ordinary

---

3. See Robert L. Millet, "What Do We Really Believe? Identifying Doctrinal Parameters within Mormonism," in *Discourses in Mormon Theology: Philosophical and Theological Possibilities*, edited by James M. McLachlan and Loyd Ericson (Greg Kofford Books, 2007), 265–81; Nathan B. Oman, "Jurisprudence and the Problem of Church Doctrine," *Element: The Journal of the Society for Mormon Philosophy and Theology* 2, no. 1 (2006): 1–19; Robert L. Millet, "What Is Our Doctrine?," *Religious Educator* 4, no. 3 (2003): 15–33.

understanding to claim that the term "vegetable" includes elephants within its ambit. Likewise, any well-informed Latter-day Saint knows that it is absurd to deny that church doctrine teaches that Jesus Christ is the savior of mankind or that the Word of Wisdom prohibits the consumption of alcohol. Such brute doctrinal facts exist even though one can make historically plausible arguments that the actual text of Doctrine & Covenants section 89 prohibits only hard liquor. Any well-informed Latter-day Saint will understand that a beer-drinking Latter-day Saint who uses such an argument to affirm to his bishop that he keeps the Word of Wisdom is dissembling.

I believe that such uncontroversial doctrinal claims exist as a matter of brute fact even when the meaning of those claims is hotly contested. For example, while all Latter-day Saints agree that Jesus Christ is the savior of mankind, they often disagree among themselves on the details—both trivial and significant—of Latter-day Saint soteriology. Such disagreements, however, do not render the original claim controversial. The distinction that John Rawls makes in *A Theory of Justice* between concept and conception is useful here.[4] The concept of justice, says Rawls, deals with a particular normative task, namely specifying rights and duties between agents whose actions need not be guided by claims of affection or benevolence. Such a concept, however, admits competing conceptions of justice. Utilitarians and contractarians may disagree violently about what justice demands. They rightly understand themselves, however, to be disagreeing about something, namely the concept of justice. Likewise, Latter-day Saints agree that Jesus Christ is the savior of mankind at the level of concept—e.g., Jesus provides something uniquely necessary in the working out of human salvation—even if they disagree at the level of conception—e.g., the relative importance of grace versus works or the merits of substitutionary versus empathy theories of atonement. In the face of these brute facts, we construct theories that make sense of the core cases, placing them in the best possible light. On the basis of these theories we then examine other teachings and practices, seeking to include within the ambit of our interpretation as much of Mormonism as possible while simultaneously casting it in the most normatively attractive terms. Church doctrine consists of the theories that emerge from this hermeneutic process. This means that the authority of a controversial teaching will necessarily be contestable. Sometimes well-informed Latter-day Saints

4. See John Rawls, *A Theory of Justice*, revised edition (Belknap Press, 1999), 9.

will have good-faith disagreements about what is or is not authoritative church doctrine, disagreements that will resist any mechanical method of resolution. This doesn't imply that there is no fact of the matter regarding the status of such controversial teachings' authority, but the inevitably contestable nature of the boundaries of church doctrine means that our discussions must be hemmed by ethical as well as epistemic norms. For example, in the Book of Mormon, the risen Christ teaches, "For verily, verily I say unto you, he that hath the spirit of contention is not of me" (3 Ne. 11:29). This is not a formula for laying to rest doctrinal disagreements. Rather, it is an injunction to avoid animosity over such disagreements.

In a 2007 *Element* article, Loyd Ericson declared a pox on the houses of both Millet and Oman (as well as a number of others), insisting that both accounts of church doctrine are incapable of dealing with the sorts of questions raised by the Bishop Bunker example with which I began.[5] Ericson's article is a detailed and nuanced discussion of the problems presented by discussions of church doctrine, but at the risk of oversimplifying his objections, it can be boiled down to two claims: first, he contends that both Millet's proposed rule of recognition and my own hermeneutic theory of church doctrine are internally inconsistent. Such proposals, he argues, claim that as a matter of church doctrine there is some method for discovering doctrine. Such self-reference, however, creates a problem of circularity. Second, he argues that neither approach can escape the problem of truth and church doctrine. Stated in its starkest form, if church doctrine contradicts itself over time—denying the Adam-God doctrine was apostasy in the nineteenth century while teaching it today would be apostasy—then how can it reflect the truth? Indeed, while his article is coy on the point, Ericson seems to suggest that the idea of continuing revelation necessarily cuts against any effort to discover authoritative doctrine and that we are best off abandoning the search. Grappling with the second of Ericson's objections helps to illustrate how his first objection is mistaken. Ericson is right to raise the issue of doctrine's relationship to truth. While I believe that his conclusions are mistaken, understanding why requires that we think through more carefully what is at stake in discussions of church doctrine.

Ultimately, I believe that church doctrine is about authority, not truth. This doesn't imply that church doctrine is false, but it does mean

---

5. See Loyd Ericson, "The Challenges of Defining Mormon Doctrine," *Element: The Journal of the Society for Mormon Philosophy and Theology* 3, no. 1 & 2 (Spring & Fall 2007): 69–90.

that the concept serves a particular theoretical and social function. Once this function is understood, many of the conceptual difficulties surrounding church doctrine disappear. What is at stake when a Latter-day Saint hears about the Adam-God doctrine and asks, "Do we believe that?" First, it should be clear that in this case the Latter-day Saint is not asking about her subjective beliefs. Indeed, if she were merely asking about her own convictions—"Do I believe the Adam-God doctrine?"—the question would make little sense, except rhetorically. After all, she could generate an answer by simply consulting her own beliefs. Nor is she asking a sociological question about the content of most Latter-day Saints' beliefs. As an empirical matter, I suspect that most Latter-day Saints have never heard of the Adam-God doctrine and would disbelieve its theological claims were they explained. Rather, she is asking a question about the church and her relationship to it. She wants to know if the Adam-God doctrine makes some claim upon her by virtue of her being a Latter-day Saint. Would her rejection of the theory alter her relationship to the Church? Is there some sense in which she is supposed to believe the theory, not simply because it happens to be true, but because assenting in some way to the Adam-God doctrine is required of faithful Latter-day Saints? It should be clear that these are questions about authority rather than questions about truth. The concept of truth may be related to the concept of authority, but it is not the same thing. Compare the question "Do we believe in the Adam-God doctrine?" to the question "Where is Kolob located?" The second question is different than the first question. It asks about the truth of the matter, but it doesn't seem to imply anything about one's duties as a Latter-day Saint. You may believe that Kolob is located in the Gamma Quadrant, and I may think that rather than being a particular star system, Kolob is a poetic device for describing heaven. You or I or (more likely) both of us may be mistaken, but unless we believe that there is some authoritative teaching about Kolob's location, our answers don't raise any question in regard to our relationship to the Church. In contrast, this is exactly what is at stake in the question about the Adam-God doctrine.

Ultimately, authority is a form of reason giving. Because philosophical modernism, which dominates our world intellectually, and philosophical liberalism, which dominates our world politically, are both based in large part on the rejection of authority, it is easy to miss this point. Modernism teaches us that the ignorant past was ignorant because people did not think for themselves but rather abdicated intellectual responsibility for their own beliefs to authority. Likewise, liberalism suggests that the tyrannical past was tyrannical because rather than grounding the legitimacy of all human action in autonomous choice, people abdicated moral responsibility for their own actions to authority. As a historical matter, the modernist and liberal view of the past is inaccurate to the point of defamation, but both myths have a powerful hold on contemporary thought. Accordingly, authority can seem a rather disreputable idea. Indeed, often liberalism and modernism reduce the idea of authority to the notion of force. The powerful image of Galileo Galilei recanting heliocentricism in the face of the Inquisition captures this sensibility. On this view, authority is the opposite of reason giving. Such a view, however, is mistaken. The conceptual structure of an authoritative reason is somewhat peculiar. Ordinarily we make our judgments about what to believe or how to act on the basis of our all-things-considered conclusions about the nature of the world. Authority, however, seeks to exclude our all-things-considered judgments about the world. Consider a simple legal example. It is illegal to drive an automobile on the freeway in excess of 75 miles per hour. I might decide on the basis of my all-things-considered judgment that the best speed is 75 MPH, and drive accordingly. In such a case, I am complying with the law but I am not doing so because I acknowledge its authority. Now suppose that I believe, on the basis of my all-things-considered judgment, that the optimal speed is 85 MPH. If I acknowledge the law as an authority, my judgment on this point becomes irrelevant. It is excluded. I drive at 75 MPH because that is what the law says.

This exclusionary structure immediately raises the question of how authority might be justified. Why might I set aside my all-things-considered judgments in the face of an authority? One simple answer is that the authority has infallible access to the truth. I acknowledge my own fallibility and go with the authority instead. Certainly, if the authority were infallible this would provide a powerful reason for ignoring my own all-things-considered judgments. More often than not, however, the connection between authority and infallibility is part of a *reductio ad absurdum*. X claims to be an authority. In order for X to be an authority, X must be infallible. X is not infallible. Therefore X is not an authority. The problem with such reasoning is that even if an authority is being justified on epistemic grounds, there is no reason to suppose that it must be infallible. For example, I accept the authority of doctors because the costs of acquiring the information necessary to make reliable all-things-considered judgments about my own health care are prohibitively high. It is not that I believe that the doctor is infallible. It is simply that I believe him to be epistemologically advantaged. I know that sometimes he may be wrong and I may be right, but on average I believe he is more likely to be correct than my all-things-considered judgments. Accordingly, in the absence of strong reasons to the contrary, I accept his conclusions, my prior beliefs notwithstanding.

This suggests that the relationship between truth and authority is complicated. It is surely the case that Latter-day Saints regard church doctrine as authoritative in part because it enjoys some privileged relationship to truth. The concept of authority, however, is not so demanding that church doctrine must be identical with the truth. Rather, Latter-day Saints are justified in letting the authority of church doctrine override their own all-things-considered best judgments so long as they believe that church doctrine, like a doctor, enjoys an epistemological advantage. This means, however, that there is no abstract conceptual difficulty in saying that some particular teaching—such as the Adam-God doctrine—was church doctrine but is nevertheless mistaken. Such a claim may make us spiritually uncomfortable. It certainly suggests that in following church doctrine we will sometimes be mistaken. On the other hand, such an admission does not render the idea of church doctrine contradictory.

Acknowledging the distinction between claims to authority and claims to truth also makes sense of the fact that church doctrine changes over time. The notion of continuing revelation means that most well-informed Latter-day Saints are comfortable admitting that church doctrine changes over time. Generally speaking, however, this change is seen as being cumulatively consistent. Hence, Latter-day Saints often imagine church doctrine as proceeding line upon line, with any innovations merely adding to previous doctrines. As a historical matter, however, such a smooth vision of theological development is difficult to defend. On the other hand, it is not strictly necessary if we are to maintain the coherence of church doctrine's authority. We may simply acknowledge that previous doctrines were mistaken. Ericson hints that the notion of continuing revelation may require some sort of dramatic new theory of truth that abandons ordinary correspondence theories of truth. I suspect that in this context Ericson wishes the notion of continuing revelation to bear too much metaphysical weight. In the end, of course, he may be correct in rejecting correspondence theories of truth. The mere fact of doctrinal inconsistency over time, however, doesn't require so dramatic a move. Rather, I can reconcile inconsistency over time with correspondence theories of truth by simply admitting that, at times, church doctrine may be mistaken as to the fact of the matter, while maintaining that ultimately the truth of church doctrine is measured by its correspondence to reality.

To a person genuinely troubled by doctrinal change over time, this discussion no doubt sounds glib. If church doctrine has been mistaken in the past, how do I know that it isn't mistaken now? How can church doctrine be trustworthy if it may be mistaken? One might respond that any mistakes in one's belief system perpetrated by church doctrine will not affect one's salvation. Indeed, one could make a fair argument that something like this claim is part of church doctrine, and seminary teachers and church leaders at a loss as to how to respond to such questions often make this claim. The mere fact that it is church doctrine, however, that following church doctrine will allow me to avoid any ultimately significant errors offers scant comfort. After all, that doctrine might be among those that is mistaken. One seems trapped in a conceptual house of mirrors from which there is no escape.

The short response to such concerns is that church doctrine cannot be used to justify its own authority. One's belief in the ultimate trustworthiness of church doctrine will have to rest on some source other than the mere fact that the doctrine asserts its own trustworthiness. This is really not all that surprising. Consider a thoroughly commonplace and uncontroversial example of a modern authority: a science textbook. I may have some theory about the mating habits of mollusks based on my own all-things-considered judgments. On the other hand, if I read a conflicting theory in an introductory biology book, in the absence of a particularly compelling reason to retain my original theory, I will abandon it. The structure of the reason giving here should be familiar. The book is an authority. How is its authority justified? One answer might be because the book itself claims to be an authority. This, however, is not why I trust the book. Rather, my reasons for acknowledging the book's authority have to do with an extremely complex set of judgments based on my sense of how knowledge in our society is produced. Indeed, it will probably be quite difficult for me to give a simple answer to the question of the book's authority. I will quickly find myself explaining why some publishers are more trustworthy than others, why some authors are to be trusted, the particular social function served by textbooks, the factors that mitigate in favor of their reliability given that function, and so on. There are two things that are worth noting about this process. First, I do not use the authority of the book's claims about its own authority to justify that authority. The justification lies outside the covers of the book. Second, the authority of the book had nothing to do with a belief in the infallibility of introductory biology textbooks. Indeed, a sophisticated reader will expect the book to contain errors.

Any answer to the question of why church doctrine is trustworthy will be similarly complicated. If asked, a typical Latter-day Saint will likely justify his or her belief in the trustworthiness of church doctrine by appealing to a mixture of personal revelation, personal experience, and reliance on the testimony of others. For example, I might be willing to trust church doctrine because I have received a spiritual witness regarding certain matters such as the Book of Mormon. I could also appeal to the positive experience of applying church doctrines in my own life. I might point out the repeated testimonies of its trustworthiness given by people whom I respect and trust. I could then point to discrete reasons for believing particular doctrines. I might, for example, be persuaded that the finitist conception of God offered by church doctrine offers an attractive way of dealing with the problem of evil. And so on. In short, while my reasons for accepting the trustworthiness of church doctrine will include elements such as personal revelation that I might not appeal to in more commonplace cases, my reasoning will be quite similar to my reasoning in other areas of life. This means that like my reasons for accepting the authority of a biology textbook, my reasons for accepting the authority of church doctrine will be idiosyncratic, complicated, and messy. Such reasons, however, will not rest on an appeal to either the authority of church doctrine's own claims about its authority or an appeal to its infallibility. Indeed, while I personally accept the authority of church doctrine, I expect it to be mistaken on some points.

It is also important to realize that I may have non-epistemic justifications for the authority of church doctrine. For example, authority can solve problems of cooperation. Consider the example of language. I might make an all-things-considered judgment that Esperanto offers a better syntactical model than English. On the other hand, in order to communicate with others in English, I must bow to the rules of English grammar, even when those rules are the needlessly complex result of mindless historical accident. Were I to try to speak using the syntax of my all-things-considered judgments, my sentences would be gibberish. Likewise, I might acknowledge an authority because to do otherwise would be to undermine a valuable social practice. When playing football, I may disagree with the referee's call. My own all-things-considered judgment leads me to believe that the ball advanced the full ten yards for a first down.

On the other hand, if I am a player, I acknowledge the authority of the referee's call because to do otherwise would be to undermine the game by being "a bad sport." The authority of church doctrine can similarly be grounded in the need to coordinate Latter-day Saint practices and maintain valuable collective arrangements.

We can now return to Ericson's two core objections. The first was that theories of church doctrine are incoherent because any claim about what constitutes church doctrine would itself be church doctrine, leading us into a hopeless circularity. This claim, however, assumes that one identifies authority by recourse to the authority itself. As discussed above, this is a mistake. If an eccentric recluse in the Texas backcountry authors an elaborate legal code, the code does not become authoritative law because it contains a clause declaring this to be the case. Likewise, an introductory textbook on biology is not an authority on the subject because the preface makes this claim. To the extent that church doctrine is about defining the scope of authoritative teachings, the method of identifying church doctrine is not itself doctrine. Rather, it is a question of social fact. The fact in question is the body of teachings and practices that in fact purport to be exclusionary reasons to Latter-day Saints. When Robert Millet offers his critieria for identifying church doctrine or when I defend my own hermeneutic theory, we are not claiming that these criteria or this theory is taught as church doctrine. We are not appealing to the authority of church doctrine to justify our claims. Rather, we are appealing to the congruence of our claims with Latter-day Saint practices, properly understood. Ericson's second claim is that theories of church doctrine fail to grapple adequately with the conundrums created by the apparent shifts and contradictions in church doctrine over time. Understanding church doctrine as being a claim to authority rather than a claim to truth per se, however, provides one with a conceptual response to this difficulty. To admit that church doctrine is fallible does not render the notion of church doctrine incoherent. It does create a problem in justifying its authority. On the other hand, we regularly acknowledge authorities of known fallibility, suggesting that this is not an insurmountable issue.

I close with a final observation about the authority of church doctrine. It is possible to present Mormonism with a pronounced anti-authoritarian inflection. Joseph Smith reported that when the angel Moroni first appeared he "quoted the second chapter of Joel, from the twenty-eight verse to the last. He also said that this was not yet fulfilled, but was soon to be" (JS—H 41). The quoted scripture reads in part:

> And it shall come to pass afterward, that I will pour out my spirit upon all flesh; and your sons and your daughters shall prophesy, your old men shall dream dreams, your young men shall see visions: And also upon the servants and upon the handmaids in those days will I pour out my spirit. (Joel 2:28–29)

This is a message of radical spiritual egalitarianism. It would be a mistake, however, to identify Mormonism wholly with this strand of discourse. Alongside this message of individual liberation to pursue personal revelation, there are equally strong claims about the importance of authority. In the earliest days of the church, for example, Hiram Page, one of the Eight Witnesses to the Book of Mormon, began promulgating revelations that he received through a private seer stone very similar to that which Joseph Smith had used in the translation of the Book of Mormon. In response, Smith issued a counter revelation, insisting that only the president of the Church could receive revelations binding upon the Church. Smith's experience with Page is as defining of Mormonism as Moroni's invocation of a nation of prophets. Accordingly, I believe that it is important for Latter-day Saint thinkers, many of whose instincts are individualistic and egalitarian, to grapple honestly and charitably with Mormonism's hierarchies and claims to authority. This requires that they use tools other than those provided by liberalism and modernism, both of which have difficulty conceptualizing authority as anything other than pathological.

That said, however, there are limits to the claims of church doctrine's authority. A full discussion of the functions served by the authority of church doctrine is beyond the scope of this essay, but I have one observation. Generally, church doctrine is a standard for teaching within and by the Church. In this respect, it is striking that while Latter-day Saints often speak of "apostasy" they seldom speak of "heresy," the sermon by Bruce R. McConkie referenced above being a notable exception. To the extent that church doctrine is involved in apostasy, we generally say that apostasy consists of teaching as church doctrine that which is not church doctrine, the paradigmatic modern case being apostate polygamous groups. Likewise, apostasy might also occur if one makes intemperate public attacks on church doctrine. To return to the example of Bishop Bunker, with which I began, he was not excommunicated for disbelieving the Adam-God doctrine. Indeed, we know that a number of Brigham Young's associates in the highest councils of the Church, such as Orson Pratt, John Taylor, and Joseph F. Smith, disbelieved the Adam-God doctrine. Rather, Bishop Bunker's apostasy seems to have consisted in what he taught in public as a bishop about the Adam-God doctrine rather than what he actually believed about it. Indeed, it is striking that apostasy does not consist in merely believing that this or that church doctrine is mistaken. While for a faithful Latter-day Saint, church doctrine certainly offers reasons for accepting certain theological claims, we generally do not use church doctrine to ferret out heretical belief. Indeed, church doctrine does not seem to be primarily about regulating the relationship of members to the Church in terms of beliefs. Rather, it polices the acceptability of particular kinds of discourse in and about the Church and its teachings. In the starkest terms, its authority is used to regulate how Latter-day Saints talk rather than how they believe. This suggests that the authority of church doctrine serves more than merely epistemic functions. Understanding these non-epistemic functions, it seems to me, would do much to illuminate the fraught question of the claims that church doctrine makes on faithful Latter-day Saints.

CHAPTER 10

Welding Another Link in Wonder's Chain: The Task of Latter-day Saint Intellectuals in the Church's Third Century

> Welding another link in wonder's chain,
> Writing new chapters of a story strange,
> God's dealings with to-day…
> — Orson F. Whitney[1]

The present is a difficult moment for The Church of Jesus Christ of Latter-day Saints. As it approaches the end of its second century, there is much to be worried about. After two generations of exponential growth, the Church's missionary program has stalled. Despite a dramatic increase in the number of serving missionaries, the number of convert baptisms is down.[2] Likewise, the Church's admirable ability to retain those born into active Latter-day Saint families, long the envy of other denominations, seems to be atrophying. More Latter-day Saint youth are abandoning the Church as they make the transition to adulthood.[3] There is also a sense of anxiety over the Church's place in society, particularly in the United States. For much of the twentieth century, the Saints thought of themselves as within the cultural mainstream, the exemplars of a widely shared commitment to the benignly patriarchal nuclear family. In the wake of the triumph of same-sex marriage and the proliferation of sexual identities in the opening decades of the new millennium, the ideal Latter-day Saint family has gone from being seen as a paragon to being seen by many as reactionary and threatening.[4] Similarly, the Church's all-male priesthood

---

1. Orson F. Whitney, *Elias: An Epic of the Ages* (Knickerbocker Press, 1904), 119.

2. See Peggy Fletcher Stack, "Mormon Growth Rate Falls to Lowest Level in 80 Years, but Ups and Downs Vary by Region," *The Salt Lake Tribune*, July 7, 2017, https://archive.sltrib.com/article.php?id=5381411&itype=CMSID.

3. See Jana Riess, *The Next Mormons: How Millennials Are Changing the LDS Church* (Oxford University Press, 2019), 4–7.

4. See "Attitudes on Same-Sex Marriage," *Religion & Public Life* (blog), *Pew Research Center*, May 14, 2019, http://www.pewforum.org/2014/09/24/graphics-slideshow-changing-attitudes-on-gay-marriage/; Tom Rosentiel, "Public Opinion About Mormons," *Pew Research Center* (blog), December 4, 2007, http://www.pewresearch.org/2007/12/04/public-opinion-about-mormons/; "Public Expresses

increases the distance between Latter-day Saints and the sexually egalitarian societies in which they often live, generating angst and alienation within the Church's own ranks, particularly among the young.[5] Finally, the Church as a hierarchical religious institution faces increased suspicion and hostility in a society where organized religion no longer commands widespread trust or respect and where the ranks of the "spiritual but not religious" are on the rise.[6]

What is the task of Latter-day Saint intellectuals in this moment? By intellectuals, I don't mean scholars working in "Mormon studies," although the groups will overlap. Nor do I mean those with ecclesiastical authority, although again the groups may overlap. Rather, I mean committed Latter-day Saints who for whatever reason feel called on to publicly discuss the course of the Restoration[7] and the place of the Church in the world. These are public discussions of the gospel, the Church, and the Latter-day Saint tradition that are both explicitly self-reflective and self-consciously religious. In short, I am talking about what might be thought of as the role of the Latter-day Saint clerisy as opposed to academics on one hand and

---

Mixed Views of Islam, Mormonism," *Religion & Public Life* (blog), *Pew Research Center*, September 26, 2007, http://www.pewforum.org/2007/09/26/public-expresses-mixed-views-of-islam-mormonism/.

5. See Riess, *The Next Mormons*, 91–108.

6. See "Public Sees Religion's Influence Waning," *Religion and Public Life* (blog), *Pew Research Center*, September 22, 2014, https://www.pewforum.org/2014/09/22/public-sees-religions-influence-waning-2/; Alan Cooperman and Gregory A. Smith, "The Factors Driving the Growth of Religious 'Nones' in the U.S.," *FactTank* (blog), *Pew Research Center*, September 14, 2016, https://www.pewresearch.org/fact-tank/2016/09/14/the-factors-driving-the-growth-of-religious-nones-in-the-u-s/; Michael Lipka and Claire Gecewicz, "More Americans Now Say They're Spiritual but Not Religious," *FactTank* (blog), *Pew Research Center*, September 6, 2019, https://www.pewresearch.org/fact-tank/2017/09/06/more-americans-now-say-theyre-spiritual-but-not-religious/.

7. According to the official style guide of the Church:

> The term "Mormonism" is inaccurate and should not be used. When describing the combination of doctrine, culture and lifestyle unique to The Church of Jesus Christ of Latter-day Saints, the term "the restored gospel of Jesus Christ" is accurate and preferred.

"Style Guide — The Name of the Church," Church Newsroom, April 9, 2019, http://newsroom.churchofjesuschrist.org/style-guide. In this essay, I use the term "Restoration" as synonymous with the "combination of doctrine, culture and lifestyle unique to The Church of Jesus Christ of Latter-day Saints."

those charged with ecclesiastical authority on the other. What is the most important challenge facing Mormonism's chattering class?

My answer is simple: finding new language in which to celebrate the Restoration.

This answer will strike some readers as strange. I imagine that a certain kind of intellectual is likely to respond by insisting that his or her role is to think critically. Surely, what we need is a clear-eyed assessment of the Church's weaknesses and failures. Only by being honest about such things can we hope to gain the trust of the suspicious outsider and the alienated member. Furthermore, isn't it vital to expose the faults and failures of the Church so they can be corrected or—failing that—so intellectuals can at least enjoy the peace of mind (and emotional frisson) that comes from "speaking truth to power"? Another kind of intellectual will respond that mere celebration is a feckless endeavor at a moment when the Church is beset by enemies and critics from both within and without. What is needed is a defense of the Church and its doctrines. Latter-day Saint intellectuals should concentrate their efforts on constructing a rational defense of the Restoration, one that will reassure the faithful, reclaim the doubter, and refute the scoffer. Precisely because of the difficulty of this moment in the history of the Church, so goes the argument, it is more important than ever that we increase the quality of our apologetics to meet the challenges we face.

I am sympathetic to both of these responses. I think faithful critics can serve an important role in the life of the Church. Likewise, intellectual challenges to the veracity of the Restoration must be met. Faith is unlikely to flourish in a world where people are told they must crucify their minds in order to believe.[8] However, with all due respect to the skillful practitioners of both genres, I do not believe that either of them represents the most important challenge facing Latter-day Saint intellectuals. This doesn't mean these activities should cease, but it does mean that such projects should be pursued only if we are confident that the far greater challenges of celebrating the Restoration in new language has been met. Ideally, both tasks should be embedded in that larger project of celebration.

Understanding why requires that we see the history of Restoration through the lens of missionary work and the absolutely central role of proclaiming the restored gospel to everything else that happens within the Church.

---

8. I borrow this image from conversations with Daniel Peterson.

In February 1829, Joseph Smith received one his earliest recorded revelations in what has since been canonized as Doctrine & Covenants 4. There, the Lord declares, "Now behold, a marvelous work is about to come forth among the children of men" (v. 1). Speaking to those "that embark in the service of God," (v. 2) he says, "For behold the field is white already to harvest. . . . Ask, and ye shall receive; knock, and it shall be opened unto you" (v. 4–5). This is the familiar injunction to proclaim the gospel. The timing of the revelation testifies to the centrality of this charge within the Restoration. This came before the publication of the Book of Mormon, the organization of the Church, or the elaboration of any priesthood hierarchy. In a very literal sense, the Restoration simply was people telling other people about the "marvelous work" of the Lord. From that time to the present, the work of proclaiming the gospel has dominated the evolution of the Restoration. Repeatedly over the nearly two centuries of its life, the Church has remade itself in the image of its most effective way of articulating the "marvelous work and a wonder" (2 Ne. 27:26) of the Lord's latter-day dispensation. This has not been the only force in Latter-day Saint experience, but over the long arc of history, it has been the most potent.

We are inclined to think of history in linear terms. We move from the distant past to the near past, to the present, and on into the future. The linear view of history lends itself to stories of progress or decline. We are either marching toward the millennium, or we are marching toward the apocalypse. One can see this in the current position of the Church. For those who grew up in the 1970s, the 1980s, and the 1990s, the dominant perception of the Church was of self-confident growth. We were expanding at a spectacular rate. Branches, wards, stakes, and temples were sprouting across the globe in places a generation or two before would have been unimaginable to a typical Latter-day Saint. Sociologists were predicting that in the coming century there would be tens of millions of Latter-day Saints, if not more.[9] The line of history pointed toward progress. Today, however, many Latter-day Saints are haunted by a declension narrative: the growth of previous years was often hollow. Baptisms are dropping. Disaffection grows. The future is bleak.

---

9. See Rodney Stark, "The Rise of a New World Faith," *Review of Religious Research* 26, no. 1 (September, 1984): 18–27; Rodney Stark, "So Far, So Good: A Brief Assessment of Mormon Membership Projections," *Review of Religious Research* 38, no. 2 (December, 1996): 175–78.

The reality is that often the history of the Church has been more cyclical than linear. During the first generation of the Restoration, missionaries reaped a massive harvest of converts in the United States and in Europe, especially in the British Isles and Scandinavia.[10] Those converts gathered to Zion, first in Jackson County and Nauvoo and later in the Great Basin kingdom of Deseret. However, over time this first great harvest of converts tapered off. The ferment of the Second Great Awakening and the missionary opportunities created by the early industrial revolution waned. Polygamy and theocracy placed the Church at war with American society and the federal government.[11] By 1901 when Lorenzo Snow, the last president of the Church who personally knew Joseph Smith,[12] died, the Church's position in the world looked very different than it had when the Lord gave the revelation launching latter-day missionary work in February 1829. Convert baptisms had slowed to a trickle.[13] While polygamy had been publicly discontinued, it had not yet been abandoned, and it would take the better part of the next decade to finally lay to rest the Saints' conflict with American society.[14]

---

10. See generally James B. Allen, Ronald K. Esplin, and David J. Whittaker, *Men with a Mission, 1837–1841: The Quorum of the Twelve Apostles in the British Isles* (Deseret Book, 1992); William Mulder, *Homeward to Zion: The Mormon Migration from Scandinavia* (University of Minnesota Press, 1957).

11. See Sarah Barringer Gordon, *The Mormon Question: Polygamy and Constitutional Conflict in Nineteenth-Century America* (University of North Carolina Press, 2002); Edward Leo Lyman, *Political Deliverance: The Mormon Quest for Utah Statehood* (University of Illinois Press, 1986).

12. Joseph F. Smith met his uncle Joseph Smith Jr. as a very young child in Nauvoo. Lorenzo Snow, however, was the last president of the Church who knew the Prophet Joseph Smith as an adult.

13. In 1901, the year of Lorenzo Snow's death, Elder Rudger Clawson reported in general conference that the Church had 310,000 members and that in the previous year it had added 20,000 members, a number that presumably included both convert baptisms and children of record. See "72nd Semi-Annual Conference October 1901," *Conference Reports of the Church of Jesus Christ of Latter-day Saints*, The Internet Archive, updated October 12, 2011, https://archive.org/details/conferencereport1901sa/page/2.

14. See Kathleen Flake, *The Politics of American Religious Identity: The Seating of Senator Reed Smoot, Mormon Apostle* (University of North Carolina Press, 2004).

The Church that emerged in the first half of the twentieth century looked like an institution whose most dynamic days were behind it.[15] To be sure, the growth of population in the Intermountain West led to a steady if modest growth in the Church, which soon spilled beyond the borders of Deseret as young Latter-day Saints migrated to the Pacific coast and further afield in search of jobs. Missionary work continued, but it cannot be said that it was particularly successful. When compared to the dramatic mass baptisms witnessed during the 1830s and 1840s by Heber C. Kimball in Manchester, England, or Wilford Woodruff in Preston, England, missionary work seemed almost moribund. An observer of the Latter-day Saint scene in the 1920s or the 1930s could be forgiven for thinking that the Church, if not in actual decline, could at best look forward to a static future.[16]

Then rather suddenly after World War II, something remarkable happened. What could be seen as a sleepy American denomination flung itself dramatically outward.[17] In the early twentieth century, Church leaders had counseled the tiny branches of Saints beyond the United States not to gather to Utah, but in 1945 there were still no non-American wards or stakes other than in the Latter-day Saint colonies of southern Alberta and northern Mexico.[18] In the second half of the century, however, Church

---

15. The best scholarly treatment of the Church in this period is Thomas G. Alexander, *Mormonism in Transition: A History of the Latter-Day Saints, 1890–1930* (University of Illinois Press, 1996).

16. For a beautifully written portrait of the Restoration at this moment by a sympathetic nonmember, see Wallace Stegner, *Mormon Country*, edited by Richard W. Etulain, 2nd edition (Bison Books, 2003). Stegner's book was originally written in the 1930s as part of the Works Progress Administration.

17. Despite the fact that the international growth of the Church after 1945 is perhaps the most influential factor on the shape of the modern Church, there are no good synthetic histories focusing on this period. Much of the story can be found in the excellent biographies of David O. McKay and Spencer W. Kimball. See Gregory A. Prince and Wm. Robert Wright, *David O. McKay and the Rise of Modern Mormonism* (University of Utah Press, 2005); Edward L. Kimball, *Lengthen Your Stride: The Presidency of Spencer W. Kimball* (Deseret Book, 2005); see also Patrick Q. Mason and John G. Turner, eds., *Out of Obscurity: Mormonism since 1945* (Oxford University Press, 2016). For a succinct summary, see Nathan B. Oman, "International Legal Experience and the Mormon Theology of the State, 1945–2012," *Iowa Law Review* 100 (2015): 719–23.

18. See, e.g., James R. Clark, comp., *Messages of the First Presidency*, 6 vols. (Bookcraft, Inc., 1965–1975), 4:165 (a 1907 Christmas letter from the First

leaders began establishing overseas stakes.[19] Missionary work was re-emphasized, becoming a standard male rite of passage in a way that it had not been previously. For the first time, the Church poured money into permanent buildings beyond the United States, most dramatically with the new temples in New Zealand, the United Kingdom, and Switzerland.[20] Missionary discussions were standardized.[21] Language instruction for missionaries was professionalized and centralized.[22] In fits and starts, through a combination of inspired vision from above and percolating trial and error from below, the Church developed a new model of what it meant to be a Latter-day Saint.

At the center of this message was the family. In a surprising move, Latter-day Saints took the theology of sealing, which had been at the center of plural marriage and the Church's grueling conflict with the federal government, and reinterpreted it in terms of the nuclear family of the 1950s. In the rapidly changing post-war world, which saw the fracturing of older models of extended family and community across the globe, this proved a potent message. Ultimately, the Church remade itself in the image of this message. The standardized teaching model that proved so successful for missionaries became a model for the correlated curriculum. The necessarily slimmed-down Church program in the expanding international stakes of the Church increasingly exerted its pressure on the institutional structure of the Church, which simplified and centralized to conserve resources. And everywhere, the nuclear family—the heart of the Church's successful missionary message—became the center of the Church.

Presidency counseling the Dutch Saints to stay in their own country); Clark, 5:199–200 (a 1921 letter from the First Presidency counseling the British Saints to remain in the United Kingdom).

19. See Oman, "International Legal Experience," 721.

20. See Prince and Wright, *David O. McKay*, 206–9.

21. This was first done Church-wide in 1961. See "History of Missionary Work in the Church," Church Newsroom, June 25, 2007, http://www.newsroom.churchofjesuschrist.org/article/history-of-missionary-work-in-the-church.

22. Efforts to train missionaries go back to the School of the Prophets in the 1830s. In 1925, the Church established the "missionary home" in Salt Lake City where missionaries received brief instruction prior to being sent to their fields of labor. In 1961, the Church established the Missionary Language Institute in Provo, Utah, which was eventually renamed the "Missionary Training Center." See Richard O. Cowan, "Missionary Training Centers," in *The Encyclopedia of Mormonism*, edited by Daniel H. Ludlow (Macmillan Publishing Company, 1992).

After a half-century of success, the model developed after World War II has largely run its course. What had proven successful in the past no longer seems to be delivering the same results. This is unsurprising. It has happened to the Church before. Periods of relative stasis and retrenchment don't mark the beginning of decline today any more than they did in the 1920s. History in this sense isn't linear. Periods of harvest give way to fallow years, which will be followed by planting and harvesting in the future. However, it is unlikely the message of those future harvests will be the same one around which the Church organized itself in the second half of the twentieth century.

Consider the message that Joseph Smith articulated in his 1838 account of the First Vision. After describing the religious revivals of his youth, he wrote:

> In the midst of this war of words and tumult of opinions, I often said to myself: What is to be done? Who of all these parties are right; or, are they all wrong together? If any one of them be right, which is it, and how shall I know it? (JS—H 10)

While the First Vision did not figure prominently in nineteenth-century missionary work, Smith was articulating a set of questions of existential importance to his contemporaries.[23] Priesthood authority from heaven and the revival of spiritual gifts spoke powerfully to these concerns. They were pressing questions to which the Restoration was an answer. They were also, however, very historically contingent questions. For most of human history and for most of humanity, the sectarian choice between competing Christian denominations has not been an existentially important choice. Indeed, even in Smith's time, it was only an important question in North America, where religious freedom and the second Great Awakening had unleashed a torrent of sectarian diversity, and on the fringes of Protestant Europe, where such controversies retained some salience. It was not, for example, a burning question to French peasants in the mid-nineteenth century.[24] It meant nothing to the farmers of Burma or Japan. Indeed, even within Britain, Joseph's questions were vital mainly

23. The First Vision did not become an important feature of Church teachings until the administration of Joseph F. Smith. See Kathleen Flake, "Re-Placing Memory: Latter-Day Saint Use of Historical Monuments and Narrative in the Early Twentieth Century," *Religion and American Culture: A Journal of Interpretation* 13, no. 1 (2003): 69–109.

24. See Samuel W. Taylor, *The Last Pioneer: John Taylor, a Mormon Prophet* (Signature Books, 1999), 146–58.

among the dissenting sects of Scotland, Wales, and the Midlands. The Twelve and other early missionaries, for example, had very little success in London or the home counties, where the established Church of England was stronger and the diversity of dissenting sects was less salient.[25] Today, this question is largely dead. Outside of a few tiny and ever shrinking corners of American Christianity, very few people regard sectarian choice as an existentially important question.[26]

Increasingly, the post-war Church's message of traditional nuclear families is becoming as attenuated as Smith's answer to the question of which church is right. It is not that concerns underlying such questions and answers are gone. People today are still interested in connecting with loved ones and forming strong families. Likewise, the sense of making one's way in a world glutted with existential options remains, even though people today do not articulate this concern in terms of sectarian choice. The language of the past, however, no longer speaks to these concerns in the way it once did. Indeed, to many that language increasingly seems alien, threatening, and distasteful. "The one true church" is a concept that appears to them as at best a gauche and flimsy response to the cafeteria of existential meaning on offer in modernity. At worst, it appears dangerously retrograde. Likewise, the benignly patriarchal Mormon family of the mid-twentieth century appears naive, reactionary, and, in a world of heightened concerns about LGBTQ+ suicide and female empowerment, positively threatening to many. Something must change if the Church is to thrive in its third century.

We can already see changes, changes that not coincidentally began in the Church's missionary program. The canary in the mine came in 2004 when the Church scrapped the standardized discussions that had been the backbone of its successful post-war expansion. In its place, the *Preach My*

---

25. See Thomas G. Alexander, *Things in Heaven and Earth: The Life and Times of Wilford Woodruff, a Mormon Prophet* (Signature Books, 1993), 96–97.

26. As one convert to the Church in the 1960s wrote:

> Because of what I'd learned from the missionaries' lesson about the First Vision, I recognized that these age-mates of mine were trapped in a nineteenth-century worldview. They thought that the "one true question" was "which church is true?" and that all the denominations were clawing at each other with different interpretations. They somehow had been freeze-framed into Joseph Smith's era.

Steven C. Harper et al., "Round Table: Saints: The Story of the Church of Jesus Christ in the Latter Days," *Journal of Mormon History* 45, no. 2 (April 2019): 54.

Gospel manual provided a much more flexible model for proclaiming the messages of the Restoration.[27] It did not, however, dramatically change the content of what the missionaries ultimately tell investigators. In the long view, *Preach My Gospel* was the beginning rather than the end of a process of finding a new model to carry the Restoration forward. We are now in the midst of that process. As it did after World War II, the Church will proceed in fits and starts as it looks for a new model of missionary success, and as in the post-war process, the messages will likely come from a combination of direction from above and trial and error from below. If we take history as our guide, however, once we find those messages they will transform the Church in their own image.[28]

Verbal agility is not necessary to the living of a good life. There is no special moral or spiritual virtue in being articulate. However, like any other gift, articulateness can be consecrated to the Lord and His kingdom. Latter-day Saint intellectuals ought to seriously consider how they can effectively consecrate their linguistic talents. The biggest challenge the Church faces today is to articulate what makes the restored gospel worth having in one's life, both for its members and for the world in general. We can no longer answer that question by saying "It reveals which church is true" or "It provides a successful way of creating a 1950s-style nuclear family." At the very least, we cannot rely on those answers if we hope to reach the majority of young Latter-day Saints and the wider world to which the Lord has commanded that we proclaim His "marvelous work." We need answers that are both compelling and comprehensible in our current historical and cultural situations.

Finding such answers is not solely or even primarily the task of Latter-day Saint intellectuals. However, for those Saints who wish to consecrate their intellectual ruminations, the most important work they can do is find new language in which to celebrate the Restoration. To celebrate something is to render it attractive and important. The new language is

---

27. See Benjamin Hyrum White, "The History of Preach My Gospel," *The Religious Educator* 14, no. 1 (2013): 129–58.

28. Indeed, to a certain extent this is already happening. It is not accidental that after *Preach My Gospel* introduced a more flexible model of preaching the gospel, the Church's Sunday School, youth, priesthood, and Relief Society curricula followed suit, providing a much looser framework for teachers at the ward and branch level. One suspects that the newly shortened Sunday meeting schedule was also driven in part by pressure to further simplify Church programs and ease the burdens on members beyond the thickly membered Latter-day Saint heartland.

required to make that celebration effective in a world where the power of old sermons and practices has atrophied. This is the most important thing that Latter-day Saint intellectuals today can do. It is important because it speaks to the central challenge facing the Church. In a sense, this is the challenge that has always been at the center of the Restoration: how does one become converted to the gospel of Jesus Christ and endure to the end? It is also the most consequential project in which Latter-day Saint intellectuals can engage because ultimately the Church will be reshaped around the successful missionary messages of the future.

What exactly might this project look like? The aim of this essay is to articulate tasks and questions, rather than any particular solution or answers. However, we have been in this position before and can look to historical analogies. In the opening decades of the twentieth century, Latter-day Saints were casting around for new language in which to convey the message of the gospel. In the nineteenth century, the most influential articulations of the Restoration had been offered by the Pratt brothers, particularly Parley P. Pratt's wildly successful *Voice of Warning* and *Key to the Science of Theology*.[29] However, by the Progressive era the cultural situation had shifted, and the Pratts' writings had lost much of their power and salience.

During this period, three Latter-day Saint thinkers sought to offer new articulations of the gospel. The most ambitious of these was B. H. Roberts, a polygamous general authority who came of age during the white-hot confrontations between the Saints and the federal government in the 1880s. Rather than simply refighting the lost battles of the nineteenth century, however, Roberts embraced the task of articulating the post-polygamous meaning of the Restoration.[30] In the early twentieth century, he sought to present the gospel as a complete intellectual system

29. See Terryl L. Givens and Matthew J. Grow, *Parley P. Pratt: The Apostle Paul of Mormonism* (Oxford University Press, 2011), 6 ("Pratt's writings, which deeply influenced other Mormon authors, particularly his equally prolific younger brother, Orson, not only helped convert thousands to Mormonism but also shaped the Mormon theological system"); see also Breck England, *The Life and Thought of Orson Pratt* (University of Utah Press, 1985).

30. Although in fairness I must note that in his multivolume history of the Church produced for its centennial, Roberts was more than willing to refight the battles of the Raid in print, defending the Latter-day Saint position. See B. H. Roberts, *A Comprehensive History of the Church of Jesus Christ of Latter-Day Saints*, 6 vols. (Brigham Young University Press, 1930).

that could accommodate modern philosophies such as Herbert Spencer's modernism and Darwinian evolution.[31] At the time, these were seen as vital currents of thought that could give the Restoration salience to his readers. During the same period, two younger writers, John A. Widtsoe and James E. Talmage, pursued similar projects. In his *Rational Theology*, published in 1915, Widtsoe presented the restored gospel as a scientifically friendly system of religion that encouraged human improvement, potent themes during the Progressive era.[32] Writing a few years later, Talmage produced *The Vitality of Mormonism*, a series of essays designed to restate the basic teachings of the gospel.[33] Writing at the end of World War I, he also emphasized improvement and advancement. In addition, Talmage linked the Restoration to the struggle against tyranny and the unfolding of human freedom, while at the same time deploring the violence and destruction of war.[34] All these are themes that would have been very much on the mind of readers who had just suffered through the Great War.

These works all repay careful reading, but inevitably they are products of their time. Some of their arguments and interpretations no longer seem plausible, while others simply feel dated. That, of course, is the point. The Restoration must be taught anew to each generation, and each generation will bring different concerns and language to the gospel. Each generation will find new insights and miss certain teachings they would have done better to emphasize. Roberts, Widstoe, and Talmage each recognized that it was not enough to simply repeat what Parley P. Pratt had taught a

---

31. See B. H. Roberts, *The Truth, The Way, The Life: An Elementary Treatise on Theology*, edited by John W. Welch (BYU Studies, 1994).

32. See John A. Widtsoe, *Rational Theology*, reprint edition (Signature Books, 1998).

33. See James E. Talmage, *The Vitality of Mormonism: Brief Essays on Distinctive Doctrines of the Church of Jesus Christ of Latter-Day Saints* (The Gorham Press, 1919).

34. For example, he wrote:

> I cannot look upon the frightful carnage and inhuman atrocities of the world war as a manifestation of the direct will of God. This dreadful conflict was brought on through lust of power and greed of gain. It sprang from an unholy determination to rob mankind of God-given rights, and to subject the race to autocratic domination. It is a repetition of the issue at stake in the primeval struggle, when Michael, the champion of free agency, led his hosts against Lucifer's myrmidons, who sought to rule by might.

Talmage, 316–1. This is a careful blending of gospel and current situation designed to appeal both to the person horrified by the destruction of the war and to the one indignant at a once aggressive and now defeated Germany.

generation or two earlier. Each, in his own way, sought to remain faithful to the Restoration. They used some language that seems familiar to a modern Latter-day Saint reader and no doubt would have seemed familiar to a mid-nineteenth-century reader. But they also spoke in ways distinctive to their times and audience. No doubt each of these works was inadequate in various ways in making the gospel live in the lives of its readers. Indeed, B. H. Roberts's speculations were so exuberant that ultimately the Church declined to publish them.[35] For our purposes, however, what is important is their willingness to engage in the central task of finding new ways of presenting the gospel message for a new historical situation.[36]

The process of celebrating the gospel today will undoubtedly look different than it did at the beginning of the twentieth century. We will use different language and even different genres. Still, the fundamental task facing Latter-day Saint intellectuals today is essentially the same as that which faced B. H. Roberts in the 1920s. For example, shortly after I became a professor, I was invited by Richard Bushman to participate in a series of private meetings of Latter-day Saint academics outside of Utah interested in the Church. In those meetings, he challenged us to identify that aspect of the Restoration we found most compelling. He then suggested that we try to articulate this in language for someone completely unfamiliar with the language of the Church. I don't think much came from our discussions, but Bushman's challenge has stuck with me over the years.[37] It strikes me as a useful exercise for any Latter-day Saint intellectual who is serious about confronting the challenges the Church faces today. It is unlikely, of course, that any such writings in themselves would matter very much, but a literature of celebration could become a resource

35. See James B. Allen, "The Story of 'The Truth, The Way, The Life,'" *Brigham Young University Studies* 33, no. 4 (1993): 690–741.

36. One might note that all three of these works were produced by general authorities. This is not quite true, as *Rational Theology* was written while John A. Widtsoe was still a professor at Utah State University. All three of these works, however, were written either at the instigation of the Church or for Church publication. They were all, in that sense, "official" publications. That said, in an era before correlation, the boundaries between official and unofficial publications were more porous than they are today. Intellectually, all these works are trying to articulate the gospel for a contemporary audience, and none of them purport to speak authoritatively on behalf of the Church as an institution.

37. I did ultimately write a personal essay in response to Bushman's challenge. See Nathan B. Oman, "A Local Faith," *Brigham Young University Studies* 49, no. 2 (2010): 163–72.

for Latter-day Saints and something that could be part of enticing others to consider the restored gospel.

To celebrate the Restoration in new language today does not mean we offer some facile bit of triumphalism or a mechanical translation of common Latter-day Saint tropes into more accessible language. Triumphalism will not render the Restoration existentially important. It will not explain to the unconvinced why they would want it in their lives. What is needed is a message that makes the Church and its teachings compelling. This means its failures and faults will have to be acknowledged and charitably dealt with. No one is interested in marble perfection. Such perfection is neither believable nor compelling for many in modern society. Fortunately, the world can be generous and open to an account of the Restoration that is willing to find the divinity within its often-broken humanity. Likewise, hostile attacks and objections to the Church and the gospel must be met. We cannot avoid responding to hard questions for which reasonable people can expect an answer.[38] Celebration may require defense as well as concession.

Truly celebrating the Restoration will require more than simple translation for two reasons. First, simple translation is impossible. Every retelling of a story changes the story slightly. This isn't pernicious; it is inevitable. However, we need to be conscious of the ways in which we are telling our stories about the gospel. Are we introducing changes that are both compelling responses to the challenges of the modern world and faithful to the divinity of the Restoration? This is a difficult process, one in which people are going to make mistakes. This need not be a problem, so long as we carry out our project of celebration with charity and humility. Indeed, the more Latter-day Saint intellectuals who are involved in this project, the less important and salient the inevitable individual errors become.

Second, a compelling account of the Restoration will likely require dramatic changes. Consider the situation of David O. McKay in the early 1950s. The Church had embarked on an aggressive program of international expansion. The goal was wards and stakes beyond the United States, centered on nuclear families bound together by the sealing power of the

38. The most tangible recognition of this need by the Church is the publication of the various "Gospel Topics Essays" dealing with such controversial topics as polygamy, the priesthood and temple ban on those of African descent, and the like. See The Church of Jesus Christ of Latter-Day Saints, "Gospel Topics Essays," https://www.churchofjesuschrist.org/study/manual/gospel-topics-essays/essays.

temple. At the time, however, this vision was in the future. Realizing it required the creation of stakes and the building of temples; remarkably enough, the Church adopted an if-you-build-it-they-will-come approach, constructing overseas temples before there were even any overseas stakes.[39] This move had a cascading series of consequences for the Church. Ecclesiastical authority moved from American mission presidents to local priesthood holders, who then became absolutely vital for the health of the Church. The emphasis on eternal families increased the importance of temples in the devotional lives of the Saints. Both these shifts placed enormous pressure on the Church's practice of denying priesthood and temple blessings to those of African descent.[40] A quarter-century after embarking on the journey charted by President McKay, the Church had been transformed, including the 1978 revelation on the priesthood. What made the post-war success of the Church possible was a willingness to imagine a future in which the Restoration would become compelling to a huge swathe of new people, even if doing so required massive transformations in the Church.

Latter-day Saint intellectuals, as intellectuals, lack ecclesiastical authority.[41] Any future they imagine as an adjunct to their celebration of the Restoration must necessarily be left implicit or merely hypothetical. Such a faithful imagining, however, is not an invitation to simply remake the Church and the gospel in our imaginations. The point of celebrating the Restoration is to celebrate *the Restoration*. This requires an effort to discern what is central and what is peripheral to the gospel. The doctrine of continuing revelation always holds out the possibility of change. Indeed, just as the idea of exaltation suggests that God both loves us as we are and also desires for us a glorious transformation into something better, God can be thought of as constantly transforming the Church to better realize the Zion promised by the Lord to the saints. This, however, presents the danger to intellectuals of simply imagining a Church in our own image, one where our ideological priors are projected onto a more palatable and about-to-be-revealed version gospel. We start as Pygmalion, falling in love with our own creation, and end in idolatry, worshipping our own graven images in a false temple. Done properly, however, imagination can be an

39. See Oman, "International Legal Experience," 721.

40. See Kimball, *Lengthen Your Stride*, 199–208.

41. This doesn't mean, of course, that intellectuals cannot occupy positions of ecclesiastical authority; they can and often do. But they do not wield such authority by virtue of being intellectuals.

act of faith and hope, so long as one remains open to the possibility of being mistaken and being given a very different future by the Lord.

Finally, one shouldn't overestimate the importance of the intellectual's task. First, Latter-day Saint intellectual life remains largely concentrated in the United States. This is a problem. There is the danger of mistaking the parochial concerns of American culture for more universal concerns. This is particularly important given the fact that even within the United States, Latter-day Saint intellectuals will likely skew toward affluence and high levels of education. Even when we self-consciously try to avoid this trap, American concerns inevitably occupy an outsized place in the discussions of Latter-day Saint intellectuals.[42] Second, in the future, the Church will need a more pluralistic message. Those things compelling and existentially important to people in West Africa and East Asia are likely different from those that move well-educated Americans. Third, while a compelling way of presenting the power of the Restoration is a necessary component of proclaiming the gospel, it is never sufficient. Ultimately, the work of the Church belongs to the Lord. It is rightly led by His prophets and apostles, not the Latter-day Saint clerisy. In the end, God's work is carried forward more by the force of charity and the power of His Spirit than through articulate speech. At best the celebration of intellectuals can help to bring people to a place where they might be touched by those things. Without them, however, the words of Latter-day Saint thinkers will "become as sounding brass, or a tinkling cymbal" (1 Cor. 13:1).

Finally, there are those who will object that the task of celebration is inappropriate for an intellectual. On one hand, one might object that what I suggest here usurps the prerogatives of Church authorities. After all, direction of the Church lies in the hands of those who hold the priesthood keys for directing the Lord's work. In the words of the fifth Article of Faith, "We believe that a man must be called of God, by prophecy, and by the laying on of hands by those who are in authority, to preach the gospel and administer the ordinances thereof" (A of F 5). Perhaps Latter-day Saint intellectuals celebrating the Restoration are merely steadying the ark and should instead await the words of the prophets.

As noted above, there is a certain spiritual danger to this project. Intellectuals, like everyone else, are prone to pride and idolatry. Furthermore, it would be wrong for covenanted Latter-day Saints to arrogate to themselves priesthood or ecclesiastical authority to which they

---

42. I am acutely aware that this is a criticism that could be leveled with some justice at the framing of this essay itself.

have not been formally called. That, however, is not what I am calling for here. Since the time of Joseph Smith, the Saints have been taught that "it becometh every man that is warned to warn his neighbor" (D&C 88:81), and we are constantly encouraged to share the gospel with others. That is ultimately what I am advocating. If missionary work means nothing more than awkwardly inviting our uninterested neighbor to church or preparing our children to serve full-time missions, then we are missing something. Rather, it should also mean throwing ourselves into the work of fulfilling the prophecy "that every man shall hear the fulness of the gospel in his own tongue, and in his own language" (D&C 90:11). Doing this, however, requires more than learning a foreign language and ritually repeating past sermons. We must do the hard work of articulating why the fruit of the tree of life is, to use Lehi's evocative word, "enticing" (see 2 Ne. 2:16) and do so in language fresh and compelling to our neighbors.

There is another objection from the opposite direction. In modern societies, the intellectual is supposed to stand outside of community as a critic and a gadfly. To celebrate, we might think, is to surrender our intellectual integrity. There are least two reasons for this stance. The first is the idea that to truly understand something, one must occupy the position of a disinterested observer. True understanding is objective, and we risk that objectivity by celebrating. This assumption, however, is a mistake. To be sure, there are often things that can be seen or understood only by virtue of a certain critical distance. However, it does not follow that only the position of the objective outsider is legitimate. There is always a bit of self-deception in such a stance, as no one is ever truly objective and outside of his or her own experiences. More importantly, however, there are certain things that can be seen and understood only from the inside. The beautiful stained-glass windows of a Gothic cathedral appear drab and colorless from the outside. Only by entering the building can their full glory be seen.[43]

Celebration, however, may strike even more deeply at our conception of what it means to be an intellectual. Socrates, the prototypical intellectual, was forced to drink hemlock because he questioned the inhabitants of Athens too closely, and there has often been tension between intellectuals and the cultures from which they spring.[44] At least since the time

43. I borrow this image from a conversation with Terryl Givens.

44. See Plato, "Socrates' Defense" in *Plato: The Collected Dialogues*, edited by Edith Hamilton and Huntington Cairns, translated by Hugh Tredennick (Princeton University Press, 1961), 3–26.

of Jean-Jacques Rousseau in the eighteenth century, Western culture has tended to exalt the alienated intellectual, the hero of the mind driven to see beyond the appearances of things to their inner essence, and in so doing, to break with the past and with convention. This stance requires a certain emotional outlook, one dominated by anxiety and estrangement from community. Often, of course, alienation gives birth to thought. It is estrangement from the familiar that causes us to reflect upon it. However, it is tempting to think that angst and hostility to community are themselves requirements of intellectual respectability. On this view, there is something intellectually embarrassing in setting out to celebrate one's native tradition.

This reaction, however, is also a mistake. It is not true that understanding or insight must always spring from alienation. Indeed, if Plato's *Crito* is to be believed, Socrates drank the hemlock only because he refused to abandon his community when given the chance.[45] His fate was tragic but marked acceptance of his native home at least as much as alienation from it. There is an alternative genealogy of intellectual life that does not rest on the supposed authority of angst. On this account, the life of the mind begins not in angst and alienation but in delight and wonder. We are driven to understand from the sheer joy of questing after truth, eternally at play amid a fascinating world. This is the sensibility that Aristotle captured with the Greek word *thaumazo*, which he suggested constituted the primal origin of philosophy.[46] In the New Testament, the word is often translated "marvel" and "wonder" (e.g., John 5:20; Acts

---

45. See Plato, "Crito," in *Plato: The Collected Dialogues*, 27–39.

46. Aristotle writes in the *Metaphysics*:

> For it is owing to their wonder that men both now begin, and at first began, to philosophize; they wondered originally at the obvious difficulties, then advanced little by little and stated difficulties about the greater, e.g. about the phenomena of the moon and those of the sun and of the stars, and about the genesis of the universe. And a man who is puzzled and wonders thinks himself ignorant (whence even the lover of myth is in a sense a lover of Wisdom, for the myth is composed of wonders); therefore since they philosophized in order to escape from ignorance; evidently they were pursing science in order to know, and not for any utilitarian end.

Aristotle, "Metaphysics," in *Introduction to Aristotle*, edited by Richard McKeon, translated by D. Ross (Nee Modern Library, 1992), 261–62.

7:31).[47] Similarly, when Nephi quotes Isaiah to describe the Restoration itself, he refers to it as "a marvelous work and a wonder" (2 Ne. 27:26; cf. Isa. 29:14). There is thus a deep intellectual pedigree in both scripture and philosophy for the idea that the intellectual's task is, to use Orson F. Whitney's words, the process of "[w]elding another link in wonder's chain,"[48] the phrase he used to describe the Restoration. At this moment, not only is celebrating the marvelous work of God a fit task for an "anxiously engaged" (D&C 58:27) mind, it is the most important work to which such a mind could be put.

---

47. See Gerhard Kittel, ed., *Theological Dictionary of the New Testament*, 10th edition (Wm. B. Eerdmans Publishing Co., 1984), 27.

48. See Whitney, *Elias*, 119.

Acknowledgments

The author would like to thank the publishers of the following pieces for permission to reprint those pieces here.

"The Disposition of Mormonism." *Wayfare*, May 1, 2025. https://www.wayfaremagazine.org/p/the-disposition-of-mormonism.

"A Local Faith." *Brigham Young University Studies* 49, no. 2 (2010): 163–72.

"Buying Jewish Whiskey." *Wayfare*, January 24, 2024. https://www.wayfaremagazine.org/p/buying-jewish-whiskey.

"From Scandal to Wonder." *Latter-day Saint Scholars Testify*, February 2010. https://www.fairlatterdaysaints.org/testimonies/scholars/nathan-b-oman.

"The Dictation of the Holy Ghost to Us: A Pioneer Day Sermon." *Times & Seasons*, July 26, 2010. https://archive.timesandseasons.org/2010/07/the-dictation-of-the-holy-ghost-to-us-a-pioneer-day-sermon/index.html.

"The Perils of Constitutional Theology." *Canopy Forum*, September 1, 2020. https://canopyforum.org/2020/09/01/the-perils-of-constitutional-theology/.

"Truth, Doctrine, and Authority." *Element: The Journal of the Society for Mormon Philosophy and Theology* 5, no. 1 (2009): 9–18.

"Welding Another Link in Wonder's Chain: The Task of Latter-day Saint Intellectuals in the Church's Third Century." *Interpreter: A Journal of Mormon Scripture* 33 (2019): 141–60.

Index

Also available from

GREG KOFFORD BOOKS

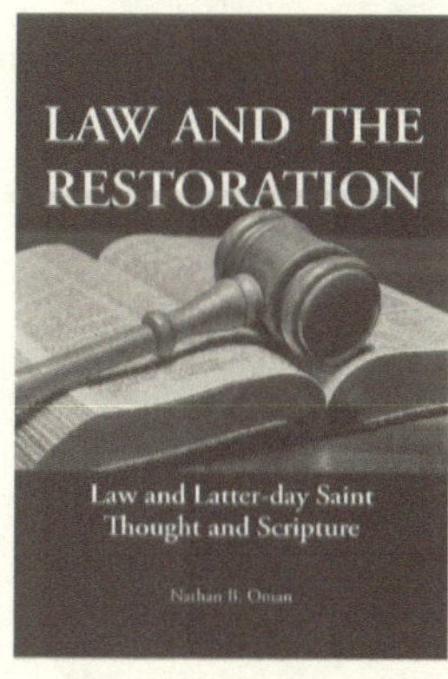

Law and the Restoration: Law and Latter-day Saint Thought and Scripture

Nathan B. Oman

Paperback, ISBN: 978-1-58958-808-0
Hardcover, ISBN: 978-1-58958-811-0

Law and the Restoration: Law and Latter-day Saint Thought and Scripture is a comprehensive exploration of the intricate relationship between legal principles and the doctrines of The Church of Jesus Christ of Latter-day Saints. Author Nathan B. Oman delves into the profound ways in which Mormon theology intersects with legal concepts, offering readers a detailed analysis of church doctrines, their authority, and their implications for members' daily lives. In doing so, Oman addresses foundational questions about the nature of church authority, the role of personal judgment, and the dynamic interplay between divine law and secular legal systems. The book is not just an academic treatise but a thoughtful discourse aimed at elucidating how Mormons navigate complex moral and legal landscapes in their quest to reconcile faith with modern societal norms.

Each chapter in *Law and Latter-day Saint Thought and Scripture* serves as a deep dive into specific aspects of Mormon doctrine and its legal ramifications. From the examination of Nephi's actions in the Book of Mormon to the contemporary debates surrounding same-sex marriage and civil disobedience, Oman provides a balanced and respectful analysis that seeks to understand rather than critique. This book is an invaluable resource for scholars, legal practitioners, and anyone interested in the intersection of religion and law, providing a rich narrative that underscores the ongoing dialogue between faith and jurisprudence within the Latter-day Saint tradition.

Praise for *Law and the Restoration*:

"A thoughtful, careful, often provocative approach to reading and interpreting Latter-day Saint history, thought, practice, and scripture."
— Conor Hilton, Association for Mormon Letters

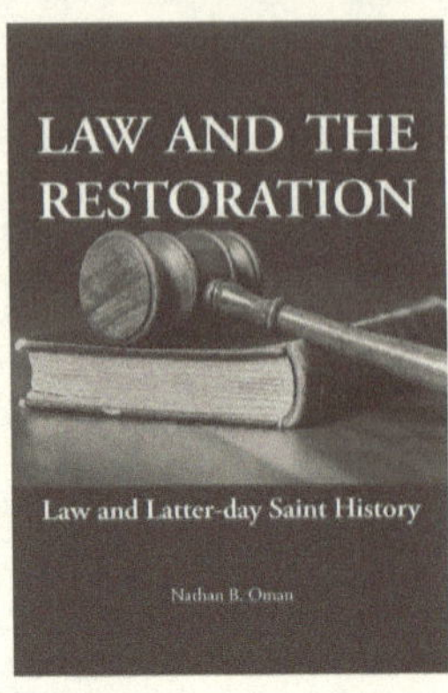

Law and the Restoration: Law and Latter-day Saint History

Nathan B. Oman

Paperback, ISBN: 978-1-58958-796-0
Hardcover, ISBN: 978-1-58958-810-3

Law and the Restoration: Law and Latter-day Saint History is a profound exploration of the intricate legal history of The Church of Jesus Christ of Latter-day Saints. In this first of two volumes, Nathan B. Oman delves into the unique intersection of law and religion, uncovering how legal frameworks have shaped and been shaped by the experiences of Latter-day Saints. Through a series of meticulously researched essays, Oman reveals the profound impact of legal conflicts and developments on the growth and identity of the Church. From the early struggles for legal recognition and the battles over polygamy to the establishment of corporate entities and the role of religious courts, this book offers a comprehensive and enlightening narrative of the Church's legal journey.

Oman's scholarly work extends beyond mere historical recounting; it situates the Mormon legal experience within the broader context of American legal history. By examining the ways in which the Latter-day Saints navigated the legal challenges posed by a predominantly Protestant legal system, Oman provides invaluable insights into the broader themes of religious freedom, church-state relations, and legal pluralism. Each chapter is a testament to the resilience and adaptability of the Church, highlighting pivotal moments and key figures who influenced its legal standing.

Imagining and Reimagining the Restoration

Robert A. Rees

Paperback, ISBN: 978-1-58958-828-8

In *Imagining and Reimagining the Restoration,* Robert A. Rees embarks on an imaginative and profound exploration of Latter-day Saint theology and culture. Through essays, poems, and midrashic interpretations, Rees sheds new light on foundational doctrines, the roles of prophetic imagination, and the divine narratives within the Restoration. He reexamines figures like Joseph Smith and Heavenly Mother, urging readers to embrace a creative and expansive faith perspective that transcends mere tradition.

This captivating work brings readers into a visionary discourse that emphasizes the power of imagination as a spiritual gift. With poetic interludes and scholarly insight, this volume is a transformative invitation to both imagine and reimagine faith, theology, and cultural belonging.

Praise for *Imagining and Reimagining the Restoration*:

"This is a beautiful book, a work of art. Enjoining us to imagine the gospel more deeply, it offers reflections on Christ, Mary, the First Vision, Heavenly Mother, and much else. Robert Rees wants to make us all gospel poets. He also seeks to make us religious critics. He gives his candid views of a broken church in need of mending, commenting on race, women's rights, sexual orientation, and earth stewardship with an imagination turned critical but still filled with warmth and good will. In the end, he invites us to imagine a kindly, loving church blessed with modern sensibilities." — Richard Lyman Bushman, author of *Joseph Smith: Rough Stone Rolling*

Every Man a Prophet

A Novel by
Stephen C. LeSueur

Paperback, ISBN: 978-1-58958-826-4

Every Man a Prophet by Stephen C. LeSueur is a powerful exploration of faith, love, and self-discovery set within the framework of missionary life in The Church of Jesus Christ of Latter-day Saints. Eddie Pedersen and Orrin Tanner, two missionaries serving in Norway, each grapple with the weight of expectation, personal desires, and the search for their true selves. Eddie struggles to reconcile his faith with feelings he has been taught to suppress, while Orrin's relentless pursuit of perfection masks a deep fear of failure. Together, they navigate a land of cold landscapes and colder hearts, striving to find meaning and connection in their spiritual calling.

Through Eddie and Orrin's intertwined journeys, LeSueur crafts a deeply human story of vulnerability and resilience. The novel delves into the complexities of identity, faith, and the universal longing to belong. As the two men confront the rigid doctrines of their religion and the unyielding truths of their own hearts, readers are drawn into an unforgettable narrative of courage and redemption. *Every Man a Prophet* is a profound tale of the sacrifices we make for faith and the truths we uncover about ourselves along the way..

Praise for *Every Man a Prophet*:

"In *Every Man a Prophet,* not only has Stephen C. LeSueur captured the lives, desires, trials, and struggles of young missionaries and their leaders better than in any other work I have encountered, **he has gifted the world with the best volume of Mormon fiction that I have read.** *Every Man a Prophet* touches hearts, opens minds, and changes lives. . . . It is a book that has the power to touch and change lives and maybe even wards, missions, and the Church." —Andrew Hamilton, Reviews Coordinator, Association for Mormon Letters

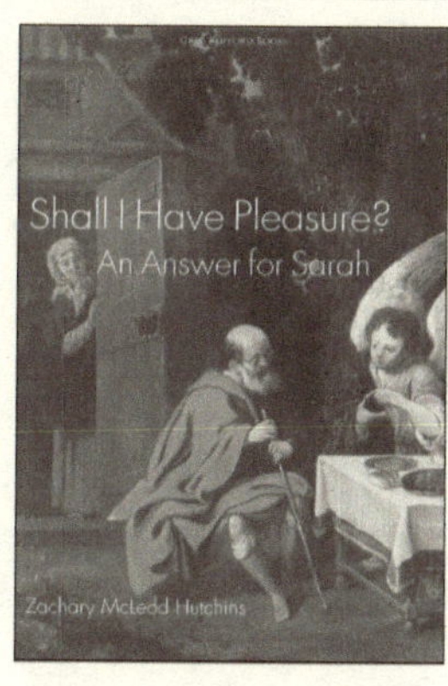

Shall I Have Pleasure? An Answer for Sarah

Zachary McLeod Hutchins

Paperback, ISBN: 978-1-58958-819-6

Shall I Have Pleasure? An Answer for Sarah explores the complex relationship between faith, desire, and the pursuit of joy through a spiritual and philosophical lens. Drawing from religious narratives, scriptural analysis, and theological insights, the book delves into how pleasure is perceived within Christian traditions, particularly among members of The Church of Jesus Christ of Latter-day Saints. Through reflective anecdotes, historical context, and doctrinal interpretations, the author challenges the tension between spiritual duty and sensory enjoyment, encouraging readers to reconcile divine purpose with the pursuit of happiness.

Rooted in scripture and enriched by personal storytelling, this thought-provoking work invites readers to reconsider long-held beliefs about pleasure and self-denial. By examining biblical stories like Sarah's incredulous laughter at the promise of joy in old age, as well as Christ's compassionate acceptance of human love and generosity, the book offers a fresh perspective on living a life of spiritual fulfillment that embraces joy as an essential part of divine intent. Through this lens, *Shall I Have Pleasure?* becomes a call to rediscover pleasure as a God-given gift intertwined with human purpose and eternal potential.

Praise for *Shall I Have Pleasure?*:

"'Men are, that they might have joy.' But many Latter-day Saints are ambivalent towards—or even skeptical of— the role of pleasure in the joy God wants for us. In *Shall I Have Pleasure?* Zachary Hutchins responds to this confusion with a beautiful and profound affirmation of the divine goodness and gift of pleasure. He invites readers to see pleasure not as a temptation to avoid but an essential and cherished part of our embodied life." — Zachary Davis, Executive Director of Faith Matters and Editor of *Wayfare Magazine*

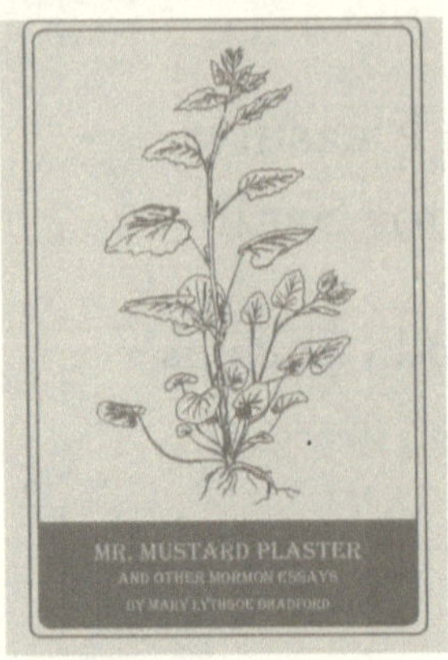

Mr. Mustard Plaster and Other Mormon Essays

Mary Lythgoe Bradford

ISBN: 978-1-58958-742-7

"Mary Bradford is the original literary 'Mormon Girl.' Long before anyone even imagined the bloggernacle, she believed that writing about everyday Mormon life—especially women's lives—could be beautiful and powerful. In her own essays, she brings unparalleled power of perception, generous humanity, and quiet humor to bear on even challenging Mormon subjects. This book is an incredible opportunity for a new generation of Mormon readers to get to know one of our faith's wise women elders. Don't miss it." — Joanna Brooks, author of *The Book of Mormon Girl: A Memoir of an American Faith*

"Mary Bradford believes that the distinctive nature of the personal essay originates from what she calls the three "I's" ("I's," eyes, ayes)—the authors' first-person perspective, their clear and rich vision, and their honest and affirming testimonies of life. Mary's own essays are true to form: her essays are vibrant portraits of a kind and loving soul, a rich and unique perspective, and a life well-lived and deeply loved." — Boyd Jay Petersen, author of *Dead Wood and Rushing Water: Essays on Mormon Faith, Culture, and Family*

"Mary Lythgoe Bradford offers her autobiography in personal essay—revealing a lifetime that bridged generations and pioneered the power of essay in Mormon literature. Since the first issue of Dialogue in 1966, Mary's wisdom and presence as an editor, writer, poet and biographer have linked us together, reaching back to women like Virginia Sorensen and moving us forward into feminism. Today at 84, Mary is still helping 'Mormon women speak.'" — Maxine Hanks, editor of *Women and Authority: Re-emerging Mormon Feminism*

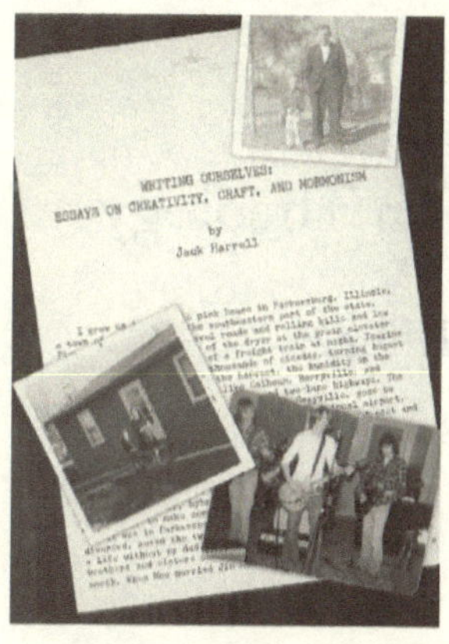

Writing Ourselves: Essays on Creativity, Craft, and Mormonism

Jack Harrell

Paperback, ISBN: 978-1-58958-754-0

Continuing a conversation as old as Mormonism itself, Jack Harrell explores the relationship between Mormonism and the writer. Mormons see the universe in mythic proportions. Their God is a creator, their devil a destroyer. This makes meaningful conflict fundamental to their worldview, and begs the terms for religious redemption, as well as the redemptive power of art. Harrell urges writers to be authentic as they embrace the difficulties inherent in the creative process. His essays blend faithful intellectual inquiry, personal narrative, research, and application to offer insights for anyone who cares about writing, creativity, and the human condition.

Future Mormon: Essays in Mormon Theology

Adam S. Miller

Paperback, ISBN: 978-1-58958-509-6

From the Introduction:

I have three children, a girl and two boys. Our worlds overlap but, already, these worlds are not the same. Their worlds, the worlds that they will grow to fill, are already taking leave of mine. Their futures are already wedged into our present. This is both heartening and frightening. So much of our world deserves to be left. So much of it deserves to be scrapped and recycled. But, too, this scares me. I worry that a lot of what has mattered most to me in this world—Mormonism in particular—may be largely unintelligible to them in theirs. This problem isn't new, but it is perpetually urgent. Every generation must start again. Every generation must work out their own salvation. Every generation must live its own lives and think its own thoughts and receive its own revelations. And, if Mormonism continues to matter, it will be because they, rather than leaving, were willing to be Mormon all over again. Like our grandparents, like our parents, and like us, they will have to rethink the whole tradition, from top to bottom, right from the beginning, and make it their own in order to embody Christ anew in this passing world. To the degree that we can help, our job is to model that work in love and then offer them the tools, the raw materials, and the room to do it themselves.

These essays are a modest contribution in this vein, a future tense apologetics meant for future Mormons. They model, I hope, a thoughtful and creative engagement with Mormon ideas while sketching, without obligation, possible directions for future thinking.

www.ingramcontent.com/pod-product-compliance
Lightning Source LLC
La Vergne TN
LVHW050951080826
845145LV00004B/1468

* 9 7 8 1 5 8 9 5 8 8 3 7 0 *